Until Trevor

Aurora Rose Reynolds

Contents

Prologue

Trevor

"You're really fucking tight!" I say, sliding through her wetness, feeling her wrap tight around one finger. "How long has it been?" I ask her, while biting down on her earlobe; damn, I love the sound she makes.

"Never," she whimpers, raising her hips up to meet my hand.

Jolting awake, I look at the time, seeing that it's just after two in the morning. "This shit is getting ridiculous," I say, scrubbing my hands down my face. Ever since the night I had my hand down Liz's pants, this shit's been plaguing me. The second the word "never" came out of her gorgeous mouth, everything stopped. I couldn't fuck a virgin, especially one that's as sweet as Liz.

"You're awake?" Anna...or Amber—maybe it's Angie—says from the other side of the bed.

"Yeah, time for you to go, sugar," I say, sitting up and wondering why the fuck I keep doing this to myself. Fucking these other women is like walking with a bottle of saltwater through a desert. You know it might look the same, but it still won't fulfill the need you have.

"Can't I stay?" She whines, running her fingers down my back.

"Nope," I say, standing and pulling up a pair of my grey AE sweats.

"So you're just going to kick me out?"

"Nope, I'm telling you it's time for you to go. Kicking you out would be bad manners."

"When can we meet up again?" She asks, putting back on her tight blue dress, wondering how the hell she slipped out of it so damn fast last night.

"I'll call you; just leave your number," I say, walking into the bathroom, knowing by the time I get out, she will be nothing but a memory.

~~*

"Yo, T!" Cash says, sliding into the booth across from me. I smirk; he uses that word at least a hundred times a day. "What are you doing here?"

I raise an eyebrow, shoving another piece of French toast into my mouth, and answering without speaking.

"You're going to Mom and Dad's this weekend? Asher is finally lifting the ban on access to July, so Mom's having a big party," he says, looking excited.

"Does he know that Mom's having a party?" I ask, thinking that if he doesn't know anything about this, he's going to flip the fuck out. Yep. I've only seen my niece twice, and only held her once, after November forced Asher to give her over.

Cash shrugs, looking over my shoulder. "Yo!" he calls, waving his hand. I look back and see Liz standing near the front door. Her long blonde hair is over one shoulder in some kind of messy braid; her strapless summer dress is fitted around her

7

perfect breasts and reaches the floor. She waves, her cheeks turning a pretty pink; then I see red when some guy pulls her in for a hug.

"And who the fuck is that?" I growl, knowing that my brothers are used to my Liz issues.

Cash shrugs again. "Don't know," he mumbles, watching them. "Yo, Liz. Come here for a second," he calls her over. The guy she's with walks to a different booth and sits facing us.

"Hi, guys," she says, her voice as soft as the curves of her body; and with me knowing what she feels like and smells like, it still fucks with my head.

"You're going to Mom and Dad's for the party this weekend, right?" Cash asks.

She looks at me, her face closing off before she answers, "I'm, um, not sure."

"Who's the guy?" I ask. She looks startled by the question for a second.

"Just a friend," she says, wringing her hands together.

"What's his name?" I ask, looking over at the guy, who has his eyes pointed right at her ass. He's younger than me by a few years. His dark blonde hair is a mess, and he looks like a fucking bank teller in his cheap-ass suit.

"Bill," she says, looking at Cash. "I'm going to go now; I might see you guys this weekend. I'll, um, let your Mom know." She turns, walking back over towards cheap-ass suit Bill, who's watching each step she takes. I have to hold myself back from going over and smashing his face into the wooden table.

"When are you going to stop fucking around?" Cash asks.

'She's fucking innocent, man," I mumble, shoving my plate away.

"So what, T? Because she's not a fucking slut bag like the bitches you normally fuck, you aren't interested?" he asks, and deep down I know he's right. She was mine from the first time I laid eyes on her at my parents' house. She was sitting outside, laughing with my mom; right then and there, I knew that she was mine. Then we became somewhat friends; one thing led to another the night of my niece's birth. I finally had her under me, and she rocked my world with the news that she's a virgin. Ever since that day, I try to avoid her.

"Gotta go," I say; getting up, I throw some money on the table, and look at Liz one last time. Great! The guy is reaching across the table, putting her hair behind her ear. My blood boils. I know I need to get over it, or step up to the plate; but either way, I need to make a move. The guy looks over in my direction; his chin lifts in warning. "Game on, motherfucker," I say under my breath, heading out the door.

Chapter 1

Liz

    I get to the front door of the club and shove it open; my stomach is full of butterflies. In all the time I've lived here, I have never been inside this club. I never thought I would even visit, let alone come seeking employment here. The inside is dark, with the only light coming from the bar.

"Can I help you?" a very pretty older lady asks. She's standing behind the bar, wiping out a glass.

"I, um, need to see Mike," I say, taking another small step inside.

"Sure, honey. Come with me," she says, walking me down a long hall. She opens the last door.

"Shannon, give me a minute," Mike says, without looking up from his computer. "November added some new program on this damn thing, and now I can't find my e-mail," he grumbles. I smile and walk around the desk, take the mouse from him, and click on the e-mail icon. He chuckles, "Hey, darlin'. How are you?" He asks in the fatherly tone that I've come to love. Mike and my dad had been best friends until my dad passed away ten years ago. After his passing, Mike had helped my mom out with my brother and me whenever she needed an extra hand. I used to pray that Mike and my mom would get married, but they were never anything more than friends.

"Could be better," I say, feeling the tears start to climb up my throat again.

"What's wrong?" Mike asks, standing from the desk, pulling me over to the couch.

"Well, I need a job."

"Okay," he says, and I can tell he doesn't know what to think. "What's going on with the store?" he asks, and I can no longer control the tears.

"Tim stole all of our money, and I can't tell my mom," I cry, doing a face plant into his chest. I don't know what happened to the brother that I used to know, the one who would come home at night to check in on me after our father passed away. We used to be close; then he moved away to school and everything changed. When I graduated from high school, I worked at a local factory for eight years, before it closed down due to the economy. Every week, when I got paid, I would put money away for savings. I have always loved to shop, and there were never any stores in town that carried anything that I would buy; so I made a plan, saved my money, and finally, my dreams were realized. "Temptations" was opened.

I sat up, looking over Mike's shoulder. "Three months ago, when Tim came to visit, he asked if he could help me out in the store. I had been working so many hours and was exhausted, so I agreed. I didn't know that the real reason he wanted to help me was so that he could rob me blind. Now he's gone, and so is all of the store's money...and mine. I can't tell my mom what happened; she's getting married in a few weeks and doesn't need the added stress from this situation. I have a private investigator looking into finding Tim and the twenty-three thousand dollars he stole, but who knows how long that could take.

I've already lost my apartment, and had to put everything I own in storage while I stay in the back room of the store. I thought that I was doing ok, until I got a notice two days ago saying that I was late paying the rent for the store. I can't afford to lose my dream," I whisper, my voice hoarse from crying.

"Shhhhh, darlin', it's okay, everything will be alright. November is not using her apartment anymore, so you can stay there; and I can give you the money."

I shake my head back and forth. "I can't take the money; it wouldn't feel right."

"I can't have you work for me, Liz," he says, as he places his right hand on my cheek. I feel bad pulling out the big guns, but I know I need money, and I can't take it without earning it.

"Can you recommend another club?" I ask pulling out my cell phone, looking like I'm going to take down whatever phone number he gives me.

"You're not going to work at another club," he says, running his hands down his face. "Jesus, I don't know what the fuck I'm thinking about doing this shit." When his eyes come back to me, I can tell that he's really torn. "Look, you can serve drinks, but you can't work on stage."

"Okay." I agree immediately. I never wanted to work on stage. I would if I had to, but the idea of taking off my clothes and trying to appear sexy just seems like a lot of work. "What's Trevor going to say about this?" Mike asks, and I looked away. Trevor likes to scare away any man who shows the least bit of interest in me. I'm pretty sure that I'm halfway in love with him already, but I know for a fact those feelings are not mutual. For a while, I thought of him as one of my best friends, until the day July was born. We ended up at his house, celebrating over a bottle of vodka. Things ended up getting hot and heavy. He had his hand down my pants, and I was so caught up in the moment that when he asked me how long it had been, I told him "never". I didn't mean I've never had sex; I meant that I had never felt that kind of fire, like my whole body was lit from the inside out. As soon as I said the word "never", he stopped immediately. I tried to tell him that I didn't mean it like he took it, but he completely ignored me. He then handed me my shirt from the floor and left the room. He has been avoiding me ever since. Which is a good thing, because I had never been more humiliated in my life.

"Trevor has no say in what I do. We don't even talk anymore," I say, hearing the sadness in my own voice.

"Yeah, alright." Mike says, running his hand through his hair. "You can start tomorrow; just ask Shannon to get you a uniform."

"Thanks a lot." I say quietly, looking at the hands in my lap.

"Don't thank me yet, honey."

"This means a lot. I know that this isn't easy for you."

"Okay, darlin'." He sighs, pulling me in for another hug. "I'll see you tomorrow. Your shift starts at nine, but come around eight; I'll have one of the girls show you where everything is, and what you need to do." He stands, taking a set of keys out of his pocket. "These are for the apartment. You can get in through the basement door that's around the back of the house. Just let yourself in.

Tomorrow, I'll help you get your stuff from storage, and get you moved in." I swallow hard, trying to control the emotions that are running rampant inside me. "Everything is going to be okay, Liz," Mike says again, pulling me in for another hug. "Now, go get your uniform, and I'll see you tomorrow."

"Okay," I whisper, taking a step away. "Thanks again, Mike; see you tomorrow," I say, leaving the office. I find Shannon back behind the bar; she gives me what is supposed to be a uniform, but feels like a few pieces of silk, and sends me on my way.

~~*

"Hey, girl," Beth—better known as Bambi—says, walking into the dressing room. When I first met her, I was a little intimidated. She's about five-nine, all legs, long brown hair, perfectly sun-kissed skin, and golden eyes. She came to Tennessee from Montana around a year ago, and has been working at Teasers ever since.

She taught me about waiting tables, pushing drinks, and smiling for a decent tip, if any. I asked her why she didn't work the stage; I mean I know for a fact that she would make a lot of money up there. But she said she was way too clumsy, and that the name Bambi wasn't given to her when she started working here. When she was little, her parents said that she could never control her legs, like they weren't attached to her body, so they started calling her Bambi.

"Is it busy out there?" I ask, putting on light pink lip gloss.

"Not really. There's a bachelor party coming in at eleven; they booked the private room. Rex said that you could help me with them. The tips should be good," she says, walking to the lockers across the room. I look in the mirror at my reflection and forget who I am for a second.

My light green eyes look brighter with the smoky eye-shadow I have on. My long blonde hair cascades over my shoulders, down to just below my breasts, which are straining the top of the black corset. It cinches in my waist, causing my hips to flare at the bottom; the fishnet stockings and black silk panties make me look like I should be going to the Playboy Mansion. It took me a few days of walking around in high heels to get used to them, at least enough to feel like I wasn't going to fall on my face every time I took a step.

It's been three weeks since I started working here. The tips are awesome, the hours are okay, and having a bed to sleep in at night rocks. The only downfall is that I have been tired a lot. Working two jobs is not easy, especially when one of the jobs you're working, no one can know about.

I met with Bill two days ago, and he gave me an update on my brother. He told me that he found out Tim had been in Alabama, but he's moved on since then, and Bill has yet to track him down again. I was starting to feel like I should contact the police, but the thought of my brother in jail didn't sit well with me.

"Okay, girl, I'm just going to change my shoes and we can go. Now, keep in mind that bachelor parties do tend to get a little crazy," she says, stepping into a pair of platform stilettos.

"What do you mean by 'crazy'?" I ask, feeling nervous. There's been a few times while I've been working when a guy would get a little handsy; but the bouncers always made sure to cut in before it could get out of control.

"Well, they tend to drink a lot more, and a lot of times, that makes them dumber than normal." I giggled. I couldn't help it; Bambi was one-hundred-percent lesbian, and thought all men were stupid. At first, knowing that she was attracted to women made it a little uncomfortable; then I realized, like a heterosexual person, she has a type, and I was not it. She smiled and shook her head. "If you have a problem, just tell me, and I'll step in."

"I'm sure they won't be that bad," I say, wondering how many people said that as their final words.

~~*

Trevor

"Yeah." I answer the phone, looking at the clock and seeing that it is just after twelve.

"Yo, T. You need to come to Teasers," Cash says, and I sit up in bed.

"It's after fucking midnight. I'm not getting out of bed to sit with you at a fucking strip club."

"Trust me, T. See you soon," he says, hanging up before I can tell him to fuck off.

"This better be good," I grumble to the wall. Getting up, I pull on a pair of jeans and a tee, and head out to my truck. When I pull up to the front of the club, I notice that, even though it's a Wednesday night, the lot is full of cars. I spot Cash standing by the door talking to one of the bouncers.

"Yo," he greets in his normal tone. He looks around before he pulls me around the side of the building.

"What the fuck?" I ask, looking around and wondering if he's in some kind of trouble.

"When you go in there, you need to play it cool, ok?" he says, and I notice he looks panicked.

"What's going on?" I ask, becoming concerned.

"When I saw her, I found Mike and asked him what the fuck was going on? He told me that she needed the money, wouldn't take it from him, and threatened to go to a different club if he didn't give her a job."

"At any point, are you going to tell me who the fuck you're talking about, bro?" I ask, crossing my arms over my chest, trying not to reach out and shake him.

"Liz," he says, throwing up his arms. "What other woman would I be talking about?"

"You're telling me Liz is in there stripping?" I ask through clenched teeth, thinking of her in there. On stage. Half-naked. With men looking at her. Now I'm seeing red.

"This is your fucking fault, T!" Cash shouts, as he pokes me in the chest.

"You tell me, how's this my fault?"

"When she came to Mike for the job, Mike asked her what you were going to think about this; she said that you don't get a say in what she does."

Well that shit burned. She was right. Technically, I didn't have a say in what she did; but she was mine, and I wasn't sharing her with anyone.

"Look, all I'm saying is be cool when you go in there. Ed's on the door tonight and said that Liz has been working a bachelor party."

"Jesus, this shit just keeps getting better and better," I mumble, running my hands over my head.

"Alright, I'm going to talk to Ed. You go in there and pull her aside; do not cause a scene."

Liz

Oh lord, I think to myself, *no money in the world is worth dealing with men like this.* For the last three hours, I have been blocking hands right and left. I lost track of how many times I've told the guys that are included in the bachelor party "no touching". I swear, the next time one of them grabs my ass, I'm going to kick them. "Can I get two more bottles, Rex?" I sigh, looking around the bar. I see Ed, the new bouncer, near the door. I squint my eyes a little, trying to see who he's talking to. Damn! It looks like Cash, but that would be crazy; why would he be here? Stupid mascara. I blink a few times and still can't see clearly.

"Cash," I hear whined from behind me, and my heart climbs up my throat. I look over my shoulder to see Skittles running in the direction of the door.

"Oh my God!" I whisper, while ducking my head. I turn and start walking back towards the private room. I think I'm about to get away, but my luck crumbles around me when Skittles plows me over, her giant fake boobs in my face.

"Sorry," she says in her fake, whiney voice. She's lifted off before I can die of suffocation. Once I'm free, I roll to my stomach and start crawling on my hands and knees towards the private room doors, hoping that Cash is not anywhere near me. I make it halfway there, when I see a pair of brown work boots in front of me.

"Excuse me," I say without looking up. I start to crawl around the owner of the boots, when they block my way again. I blow my hair out of my face, becoming frustrated by the person in front of me. Can't they see I'm trying to get away? The person squats down, and I see denim-covered knees; then fingers are under my chin, lifting my face. "Crap," I whisper, when I see Trevor's brown eyes looking into mine.

"We need to talk." He says quietly, and I can see by the look in his eyes that he's pissed.

"No, we don't need to talk," I say, trying to stand. Who knew that getting up off the ground when you're in high heels was so much work? I fall forward, my hands landing on his chest, and his going to my waist, steadying me. "Thanks," I mumble. Not the first time wishing I knew magic, so I could cast a spell to stop whatever power it is that he has over me. I hate that my body craves his touch; I hate even more the fact that I crave it, knowing that he's a big jerk. As I steady myself, I don't look at his face again as I take a step around him.

"We need to talk," he repeats, and I pretend that I don't hear him. I continue walking towards the private room, where I know kick-ass Bambi, the man-hater is. "I'm not going to tell you again, baby," he says, coming up behind me, pulling my back to his front.

"Let me go, Trevor." I say quietly, trying not to cause a scene. He doesn't say anything, but wraps his arms around my waist, walking me with him down the hall towards Mike's office. I start to struggle to get away, when I see the door getting closer. I don't want to talk to him, and when I had wanted to talk to him, he didn't want to listen. I squirm and almost make it free of him, when he gets Mike's office door open, shoves me inside, and slams the door behind him. "Great. Just great," I grumble to myself, as if I had a chance of winning that battle. I put my hand on my hips, ready to give him some major attitude, when he takes my breath away.

"Jesus, you look beautiful!" he says, walking towards me with a look of hunger in his eyes. I start walking backwards, caught off guard.

"Um...thanks," I say, looking over my shoulder and noticing that I'm heading towards the couch. Knowing that I don't want to be near any horizontal surfaces and Trevor at the same time, I start making my way towards the desk, hoping that I can put it between us. "Stop," I say, holding out my hand when I see how close he is to me. He stops, and I roll the desk chair between us to block his way. "Okay," I breathe; he raises his eyebrows and crosses his arms over his chest. I wish he wasn't so good looking. His dark brown hair is cut low to his scalp; his brown eyes are made more beautiful with the long lashes that frame them. His jaw is square, and like always, it looks like he needs to shave; the dark growth around his mouth makes his full lips stand out even more.

He's a lot taller than my five-five-and-a-half; even in the six-inch heels I'm wearing now, he towers over me.

His eyes rake over me, and his mouth goes into a flat line. "What are you doing, Liz?" I look around Mike's office, avoiding his question. I notice that I'm not too far from the door; I might be able to make it there before him if I kick off my shoes. "Try it and I'll spank you." Okay, really? I'm ignoring that comment. I slide my foot out of one heel, but don't put my foot down. I don't want him to notice what I'm doing until the last possible second. "Talk to me," he growls, and I glare at him. "You're working at a fucking strip club for God's sake; what the fuck is going on?" he roars, leaning towards me.

"It's none of your business," I say, crossing my arms over my chest.

"What? None of my business?" he asks.

"Let me clarify that," I say, pausing to put my hands on my hips, trying to balance in my one shoe. "It's none of your *damn* business."

"I've had my hands down your pants. I know what you sound like when you're going to come."

"Well, mister, you don't." I look towards the door again.

"Don't what?" He asks, smirking.

"Know what I sound like," I say, getting tired of this game he's playing.

"We can take care of that right now," he says. I look at him like he's crazy, and shake my head.

"Um, no thanks," I say, looking towards the door, wondering where the heck someone—anyone—is.

Don't they realize that I'm missing? Shouldn't they be looking for me?

"Look, I'm sorry, but I just couldn't do it. You're too sweet. That's why you shouldn't be working here."

"Well, too bad. I need this job, and I'm keeping it."

"You're innocent, Liz, a fucking virgin, and you want to work at a strip club?" he growls.

"First of all, it's none of your business, but I'm actually not a virgin. Second of all, there was not one single question on my application for this place about my sexual history," I say, completely pissed off.

"Who the fuck have you been with since we were together?" he asks. I can see his face turning red.

"No one! Geez, Louise," I say, waving my hand in front of me.

"How exactly do you go from you having never, to now?" He asks, looking as confused as his question sounds.

"I never said that I was a virgin," I snap. "You chose to hear that, and then you walked away, completely ignoring me when I tried to explain it to you. Which, by the way, was pretty damn embarrassing." I say, crossing my arms over my chest, feeling almost as embarrassed as I did the night that we were together.

"Fuck me," he whispers, running his hands down his face.

"Look, I really need to go. I'm sure Bambi is freaking out; I left her with a bachelor party," I say, looking towards the door again, ready to run for it.

"We're leaving," he says, taking a step in my direction.

I stop and look at him. "No, I'm working. We're not going anywhere."

"You just resigned; it's time for you to go home."

"Wow, you got this whole caveman act down pat, don't you?" I say, slipping back into my shoes. There is no way that I'm going to let him intimidate me.

"You come with me, or I'll tell your mom what you're doing during your free time," he says, and I feel all the color drain out of my face. My mom can be pretty cool, but if he told her I was working here, I would have to explain why I needed a second job; I can't see her being very understanding about that.

"I never thought that I could hate you, but you just proved me wrong." I say quietly, as tears start to fill my eyes. My shoulders slump, and I start walking towards the door.

"Where are you going?" he asks me as I open the door. I don't even turn around to answer him.

"Getting my stuff and going home, Trevor. Just like you wanted me to." I see Bambi in the dressing room when I get there; she's in front of the mirror adding more lip gloss.

"Hey! Ed said you were talking to someone when I went to look for you; is everything okay?"

"Um, not really. I'm leaving," I say, pulling my pink gym bag out, and shoving everything that's mine into it, while trying to avoid looking at Bambi.

"You're leaving?" she asks, and I can feel her as she comes to stand next to me.

"Something came up and I need to go; I'm sorry for leaving you with those guys. I'll talk to Mike on my way out so he can send someone else to help you," I say, pulling my hoodie on over my top, stepping out of my heels, and into a pair of black, high-top Converses.

"I don't care about that. I'm worried about you and why you're leaving," she says, hugging me.

"Ready?" Trevor asks, sticking his head in the room. We both turn our heads in his direction at the sound of his voice.

"What the fuck, dickwad?" Bambi yells. "Get the fuck out of here; can't you read? This is a women's only area, and unless you want me to give you a vagina, you need to leave." She walks over, slamming the door in a stunned Trevor's face. I giggle; no matter how bad this is right now, she made it worth it. "Are you leaving with that douche?" she asks, walking back towards me.

"No, he just came to tell me something," I say, walking towards the door.

"Call me and let me know you're okay," she says, and it makes me want to cry. She has made working here fun, and has become a pretty good friend.

"I'll call you tomorrow," I say, opening the door, walking right past Trevor, Cash, and Mike.

"You okay, darlin'?" Mike asks, putting his arm around my shoulder.

"Yeah, I'm just gonna go home. I'll see you tomorrow for breakfast; and thanks for the internship."

"I'll see you then, and we can talk," he says, squeezing me to his side.

"Great," I mutter, walking out into the parking lot to my Charger. I open my door and throw my bag across, into the passenger seat.

"Hey, we need to talk," Trevor says, turning me around with his hand on my waist.

"No, Trevor, we don't need to talk."

"We're friends, Liz. This isn't you; I just want what's best for you," he says, trying to pull me into him. I take a step back, get in my car, and slam the door, engaging the locks before he can stop me or open my door. Turning on the car, I rev the engine, then roll down my window an inch.

"Just so you learn a lesson from tonight, I'm going to clue you in; you know, since were friends and all." I say sarcastically. "First of all, *friends* ask each other about their lives. Second, a *friend* would wonder what circumstances would cause someone to work somewhere that they never would have before. And last, but not fucking least, a *friend* would never threaten another *friend*." With my parting words, I rev my engine and let the gravel fly behind me. My car fishtails right before I get to the stop sign. I turn up Nickelback's *"Animals"* on my car stereo, stick my hand out my window, and flip Trevor off. As soon as I roll up my window, tears start sliding down my cheeks from the sadness and anger I'm feeling. I trusted Trevor at one point, and just like my brother, that trust was not earned, and now I'm more stuck than I was before. I have to find a way to earn the money that I need to save my business, without getting my mom involved and making my brother do time.

Trevor

"Well, I have to say, that went well; don't you think, *friend*?" Cash asks, while patting my chest before he walks off. I'm completely stunned, stuck in place, wondering what the fuck just happened. "Yo! T, are you coming, or what?" He shouts from across the parking lot, snapping me out of my stupor. I lean my head back, looking up at the night sky. Seeing a shooting star, I make a wish; I close my eyes, let out a breath, and walk to my truck, knowing tomorrow is a different day.

Chapter 2

<u>Liz</u>

Waking up to the floor creaking above me, I roll over and look at the clock, seeing that it's just after nine-thirty. I know that Mike is eating breakfast, then going to sleep. Part of me wants to avoid going upstairs; I want to hide under the covers of my bed like I did when I was little, and pretend that my life is perfect and normal. I want to pretend that Trevor didn't threaten to tell my mom on me, that my brother didn't steal my money, and that I wasn't at risk of losing a dream that I have worked so hard for. I toss the covers back, jump out of bed, grab a pair of pink sweats from the floor, pull them on, and head up stairs.

"Hey, darlin'," Mike says, as I come through the basement door.

"Hey," I mumble, heading to the coffee pot.

"We need to talk about last night, darlin'."

"I know," I say, pulling a mug down, pouring coffee, cream, and two Splendas into it. I hop up on the counter and take a sip of coffee. "I'm sorry about last night. Trevor caught me off guard, and I was upset. I didn't mean to take it out on you."

"I know that you're mad at him, but he really is just trying to look out for you." I almost tell him that he's really only looking out for himself. Just like everything with Trevor, it's all about him. Instead, I bite my tongue and nod my head. Who knows? Maybe in the alternate universe that Trevor lives in, he really is helping me. Too bad for me, my business loan, car loan, and shop rent doesn't exist in his universe.

"Your dad was my best friend," Mike says, his face getting soft. "The day you were born, he was overjoyed. I was depressed; I never really thought of being a father. But when I found out that Susan was pregnant, I knew that I would be the best dad I could be. Then Susan took off, and I had no way to get November back. I had no idea where her mom had gone with her. So when your dad told me that he and your mom were expecting a little girl, I was jealous. I wanted that for myself. Then you were born, and your dad handed you to me and told me that I was going to be your godfather. He said he knew just by looking at you, he couldn't imagine having someone take you from him, so he was going to share you with me." He chuckled, rubbing his jaw. "Your dad was a good man and a great friend." I nod my head in agreement. I can feel tears stinging my nose again. "I'm giving you the money, Liz. The money Tim stole from you and your mom. No more bullshit about working for it. You did work for it, and then it was taken from you. So now, I'm going to do what your dad would have done. I'm giving it back to you." I start shaking my head. "If Tim turns up, he owes me, Liz; you're not doing this shit anymore. I'm helping you out. You can stay downstairs in the apartment as long as you want. Now, I'm going to bed. I left the check in an envelope on the table near the door. Make sure you take it." He kisses my forehead, leaving me speechless sitting on the counter.

"Hey Mom," I say, walking into Temptations. After Mike left this morning, I pulled myself together, finished my coffee, and picked up the check from next to the front door. I wrote Mike a long thank you note, not only for the money, but for always being there for me after my dad passed away. Then I went downstairs, showered, and got dressed in a pair of wide leg jeans, a black ribbed tank, and my black cowboy boots. Around my hips, I looped a wide black belt with a huge turquois buckle that I also sell in my store. I stopped at the bank on the way to the store and deposited the check. I paid my business loan three months in advance, the same with my car payment. Then I called the owner of the building we lease our shop from and paid the back rent and a few months in advance.

"Hey, honey. These came for you." She points to a large vase of assorted lilies. I noticed the smell when I walked in the store but thought they were from her fiancé. I walk toward the counter and find a card. My heart is in my throat when I open it, wondering if they're from Trevor. My name is written in a woman's handwriting on the outside of the card. I slide my finger under the edge of the small envelope, pull the card out, and flip it over.

"Crap!" I mumble. The flowers are from Bill; not that Bill isn't a nice guy, but the thing is, he just does nothing for me. When I hired him to find my brother, I tried to make things clear that this was going to be a completely professional relationship; but he is constantly asking me out, or flirting in a way that makes it clear that he's interested.

Bill was my first. All my life I have been reading romance novels. Those stupid books ruined me. I've always wanted that fire that every book I ever read talks about. There was no fire with Bill; and afterwards, I thought that the fire described in books was a whole bunch of made up mumbo-jumbo until I was with Trevor. Then I found out that not only is it real, it is consuming. Unfortunately, only he could give me that feeling, but I'm not the only one to give that feeling to him. The women in town are constantly talking about him or his brothers, and the amount of women they go through. Well, all except Asher. He was just as bad as them until he met November; she turned his ass upside-down. Now they're one of those couples who are constantly touching or whispering to each other, completely head-over-heels in love; and now that they have their daughter, they are even more in love. I couldn't be happier for them. But naturally, I'm jealous. Who wouldn't be? Really, what woman wouldn't want one of the hottest men this side of the Mississippi banging down your door, confessing his undying love, while begging to take care of you, and then giving you a perfect family?

"Well, who are they from?" my mom asks, and I look up at her hopeful face. I know that she thinks I need to find a man. She had me at twenty, and was with my dad for two years before that.

"Bill," I say, wondering if I should give him a shot. I'm sure thousands, no *millions*, of women are in relationships with people who don't cause them to catch fire with just a look.

"Oh," she says, her face falling. "I thought they were from Trevor; he is such a nice boy." I shake my head; my mom has no idea the kind of guy Trevor really is.

"I'm going to unbox the new shipment and stock the shelves. Let me know when you're going for lunch and I'll come watch the front for you," I say, kissing her cheek.

"Okay, honey," she says, sliding my hair behind my ear and kissing my forehead.

I am in the back room going through the new shipment, when my mom comes back to tell me she is going to lunch. I make my way to the front of the store, carrying some stuff to put on display, when the bell over the door goes off. I turn my head to see Trevor standing near the cash register. I raise an eyebrow at him, wondering what the heck he's doing here.

"You got time to talk?" he asks, while looking around. I take a deep breath, let it out, and shrug my shoulders. "I talked to Mike this morning, and he told me what happened with your brother." I feel my chest squeeze. I didn't want anyone to know about what my brother did. "Why didn't you tell me about it?"

"Seriously?" I ask, glaring at him.

"Shit, I know I fucked up. I just—" He stops talking and runs his hands over his head. When his eyes come back to me, they look confused. "You're you; I care about you."

"You, Trevor Mayson, are full of it."

"What?"

"You don't care about me, Trevor," I say, turning my back on him, going back to putting out the new stock.

"We were good together," he says next to me. I look over at him, my eyebrows drawing together.

"What are you talking about? We were never together." I shake my head. "We hung out. I had considered you a friend; then we got drunk, fooled around, and you showed me that I was nothing but just another woman, just like all the others." I blow a piece of hair out of my face, feeling myself turn red from embarrassment. "Now if you would just leave and not talk to me any more like you did before, that would be great," I say, turning around to finish what I was doing.

"Why's this Bill sending you flowers?" I look over and see him standing in front of the flowers, looking at the card.

"What's with you?" I walk over and snatch the card out of his hand.

"You're coming with me to go see July Saturday when you get off." I look at him like he has lost his damn mind. He shrugs. "I already told Asher that you would be there." "Well, then, I guess you have to call and tell him that you were confused," I snap, just as the shop door opens and my mom walks in.

"Oh! Trevor, honey, so nice to see you," she greets, and he bends low to kiss her cheek.

"You too, Mrs. Hayes. I was just coming to remind Liz about our plans for the weekend."

"Plans?" my mom asks.

"We're going to see July, then to dinner afterwards," Trevor tells my mother. Her face lights up like a Christmas tree, and she looks over at me smiling.

"Oh, that's wonderful," she claps—yes, claps— and I want to grab Trevor's ear and haul him out of the store.

"Thanks for the reminder. I'll text you if something comes up and I can't make it." I say, walking to the door and opening it.

"If you can't make it, then I'll just pick you up after," he says, running his fingers through my hair. "Just don't forget your overnight bag," he says, leaning closer. I know my jaw hit the floor. I look over at my mom and she's beaming. I can see the sun shining from inside her. I look back at Trevor, ready to kick his ass for making my mom think that there is something between us that isn't there. Then I feel his mouth on mine. I try to pull away, but his hand is in my hair at the back of my neck, holding me in place. He licks my bottom lip, then bites it softly. My hands had gone to his chest to shove him away, when I feel his other hand at the underside of my breast; my mouth opens, his tongue touches mine, and his taste fills my mouth. My brain is no longer in control. I kiss him back, one hand fisting his shirt, the other at the back of his head, his hair scraping against my palm. His mouth leaves mine; pulling me deeper into him, I feel his lips near my ear. "I forgot how much I love your mouth baby," he groans, and I feel heat hit my face. Not only did I just do that in front of my mom, but he has the power; all he has to do is touch me and I'm his. "I'll see you Saturday," he says, pulling away. My brain is total mush; all I can do is nod. He says goodbye to my mom and leaves the store, with me standing right where he left me.

"I'm surprised that this place didn't catch fire when he kissed you," my mom says, beaming at me. I bite my lip, asking myself, not for the first time, what just happened.

"Um…"

"I mean, I'm your mom, but it looked like that boy knew how to kiss."

"I ugh…"

"I know that he's got a reputation with the ladies, but seeing him work, well, now I know they're not just rumors," she says, fanning herself.

I take a deep breath, closing my eyes. "Mom, please don't get all excited, okay? Trust me when I tell you that nothing is going to come from this."

"If you say so, honey," she mumbles, going behind the counter. I walk to the back room of the shop, close the door, and scream at the top of my lungs, trying to get all the frustration I was feeling at that moment out. Once I'm done, I go back to stocking the shelves, trying to keep myself busy enough to forget about Trevor and his kiss. This doesn't work, so I call Bambi, hoping that she can make me forget about Trevor. Unfortunately, she wants to talk about him, why he was there, and what happened when I left the club. I explain the best I can without telling her too much. Then I call November, and she also wants to talk about Trevor, and how he called Asher and told him that we would be there Saturday to spend some time with July. It was like the world is against me. Nothing helped me forget about him; even after I get home, I can still feel his mouth and hands on me.

~~*

"Do you want a beer?" Bill asks, coming to stand next to me. He called me this morning and asked if I wanted to go to a bonfire with him. Normally, I would avoid things like this because the women I went to school with act like they are *still* in high school. Being twenty–five, I think that it's a little crazy to still whisper and talk crap about people behind their backs, then play best friends when they are standing in front of you. In school, I was a nerd...a big one. I had braces, my hair was short, and I dressed like a boy. When my dad passed away, my mom checked out; I know she tried, but it was hard enough for her to get out of bed most days. I think she figured that we didn't need her, and that we were old enough to get up and go to school; and let's not forget: cook for ourselves, do our laundry, or clean up after ourselves. Things weren't easy, but I never wanted to be the one to rattle our fragile existence; so instead of telling my mom that I needed clothes, I would borrow my brother's; instead of saying I needed a haircut, I would just take the scissors, and cut my hair short enough that I didn't have to think about it.

My whole high school life, people called me Liz the Lez, Lezzy Liz, or some other stupid nickname that rhymed with Liz. In school, I had one friend; her name was Cassy, and when she moved senior year, I was on my own. Tim had gone off to Seattle to school, and my mom was working part time at a bar. When she wasn't working, she was sleeping. I think that was one of the worst years of my life. Then on graduation day, when I walked across the stage, I looked down and saw my mom. She was looking at me, her eyes blood shot, and I could see regret written all over her face. After graduation, we went home; she ordered pizza and made me a cake. We pigged out, and she told me that she was sorry for not being there for me, but that she would make it up to me every day from then on. She stuck to her promise, and I truly couldn't ask for a better mom. She helped me find myself, while finding out who she was without my dad.

"So do you want one?" Bill asks again, and I look over at him and shake my head. I'm tipsy already, and want to go home. It doesn't help that I never wanted to be here to begin with. But standing out in the cool night air in a tank top, listening to some girl talk about how she's going to try and trap one of the Mayson boys by getting knocked up, and that she doesn't care which one it is, just as long as one of them is her baby-daddy, I know I need to go home. "Here, take my hoodie," Bill says, taking off his red college hoodie and putting it over my head. "You look so cute," he says, leaning in like he's going to try to kiss me, so I lean back.

"I'll be back," I mumble, looking away from him and towards where my car's parked.

"Do you want me to come with you?"

"No, its fine. I'll be right back," I say, leaving the warmth of the bonfire, heading in the direction of my car. I have no idea what I'm doing, but hiding seems smart at this point. "Me and my stupid, stupid brain, thinking that I could go out with Bill and forget about Trevor. Ha! That's a joke, if I ever heard one. Oh no, what if it's like, some weird virus, and I'm like, addicted to him? I mean, that girl was going to trap him, or any Mayson by having a baby. What if I become crazy and try to do that too?"

"Who are you talking to?"

I scream, jumping back, and end up falling on my ass. When I look up, I see the cause of all of my problems standing over me. "You scared the crap out of me." I glare at him; he ignores me, pulling me up.

"How's your bottom?" he asks, pulling me closer.

"Stop!" I yell, as he starts patting my butt where dirt and twigs are now stuck.

"You're dirty, baby; just trying to help," he says, holding up his hands in front of him.

"It's fine. I'll get it," I grumble, dusting myself off. Trevor leans forward and his eyes narrow.

"Whose sweatshirt is this?" he asks, tugging at it with a look of disgust on his face.

"Bill's," I say, starting to walk around Trevor; but before I can make it two steps, I'm upside-down over his shoulder.

"What the hell are you doing? Put me down right now." I kick my feet, trying to get him to put me down, but nothing is working. Then I'm right side up, but sitting on the tail of his truck. "Seriously, what the hell is wrong with you?" I ask, then Bill's sweatshirt is gone. "Hey, I was wearing that!" Suddenly, I'm wearing a hoodie that smells like Trevor; my senses go into over drive. "What are you doing?" I repeat, as he pulls my hands through the sleeves of his grey work–hoodie. Oh great, the Mayson logo on it, along with his name.

"You smell like that douche," he says, looking irritated as he rolls the sleeves up on his sweatshirt. "Are you drunk?" he asks, leaning forward and looking into my eyes.

"I'm not drunk," I whisper; having him this close and smelling him all around me is playing havoc on my intoxicated state.

"I'm taking you home," he pulls me off the back of his truck and leads me to the passenger side.

"I'm staying here," I tell him, trying to pull free. I don't want to stay, but I really don't want to go with him.

"You're drunk. It's late and I'm taking you home."

"I'm not drunk. I can't leave my car here, plus I drove Bill."

He starts laughing, looking around. "So you're here with that guy? He let you drive here, and he let you wander off drunk?" I see his jaw clench.

"Last time I checked, there wasn't a law about women driving; and not only that, but I didn't wander off. I'm not a dog who needs to be on a leash," I say, becoming angry.

"I never said you were; I'm saying that if he was with you, then he should be making sure that you're okay."

"I was going to my car; I wasn't going to wander in the woods, Trevor."

"Just let me take you home, okay?"

I let out a long breath. "I'll have Bill take me," I tell him, trying to compromise.

"No, I'm taking you."

"I drove him here. I can't leave him stranded out here."

"I'm sure that Tammy will give him a ride." I scrunch up my nose, wondering who Tammy is, and why she would give Bill a ride. Then I look in the direction of the bonfire and see Bill sitting on a large boulder with a red-haired girl in a very, *very* short skirt, who I assume is Tammy, straddling his waist.

"Okay! So she will give him a ride, but I still need to get my car home." Trevor looks at me like I should be crying over Bill and Tammy, but I honestly couldn't care less.

"I'll have Cash come and take your car home."

"Okay, but aren't you going to miss out on the party?" I say, looking around.

"No, Mike told me you were here, so when you didn't answer my calls, I came to make sure that you were okay."

"You came all the way out here to check on me?"

He shrugs, looking a little uncomfortable. "It's what friends do; I'm going to be your best friend."

"I don't want you to be my best friend. I don't really even want you to be my friend," I say, wondering if I've been sucked into Trevor's universe by some unseen force.

He mumbles something that I can't hear and I raise an eyebrow, signaling for him to speak up. "Can we fight about this tomorrow?" He scrubs his hands down his face. I can see the tiredness around his eyes when they come back to me. "I'm beat. I had a long day and I just want to go to sleep."

"Fine," I sigh, climbing into his truck, feeling bad that he came here to check on me when he's so obviously exhausted.

"Now, what are you doing?" I ask, batting his hands away.

"Putting your seat belt on."

"I can manage my own seat belt," I tell him, pulling it out of his hands and locking it in place. He finally climbs in behind the steering wheel, pulls out his phone, calls Cash, and asks him to take my car home. Cash and Nico promise to drop it off at Mike's by morning, and to leave the keys in the cup holder. I am not worried; in the country, no one steals cars, and everyone I know leaves their keys in their car overnight. Half way home, my phone rings, and I see that it's Bill calling. I answer on the second ring.

"Hey," I say, putting the phone to my ear.

"You ditched me, and someone saw you driving off with Trevor Mayson."

"Trevor's taking me home. I'm tired," I tell him, which is not a lie. "I saw you with Tammy and didn't want you to leave just because I wanted to go home."

"She came on to me, I swear; I tried to push her off." I roll my eyes, wondering how stupid he thinks I am.

"It's fine. I told you, we're just friends; you can do whatever, or whoever, you want," I reply, looking over when I hear Trevor chuckle.

"You have my sweatshirt," Bill says. I can hear the agitation in his voice.

"You said you had some new info on my brother, right? You can tell me tomorrow when I drop off your hoodie."

"Yeah, all right. Look, just call me when you get home, okay? I want to know that you're safe."

"I'll be fine; just go have fun," I say, hanging up.

"What's the deal with you and that guy?" Trevor asks.

"We worked together at the Tollie factory when it was open. We dated for about a year. When the factory shut down, he moved and started working for his uncle, who's a private investigator. We agreed to see other people, but were always friendly. Then when I found out what Tim did, I called him and asked him to help, and he agreed," I say, laying my head against the window, watching the moon follow us off in the distance.

"So, he's your friend?"

"I guess."

"I should have talked to you," he says, and I couldn't agree more. I thought that we were friends. We'd spent time together, we laughed, I could call and talk to him about anything, and he was there for me. Then it was like I wasn't worth anything to him when he thought I was a virgin. He wouldn't talk to me; he ignored me when we were in the same place. And worse, if we were out, he always had a girl on him. And any man that came and introduced himself, he would send someone over to make him leave me alone, even if it was the girl that he was talking to. It was like he was trying to say that I wasn't good enough to have a relationship with anyone.

"Yeah, you should have talked to me," I whisper, looking back out the window, ignoring him the rest of the ride home. "Thanks," I say when we pull up in front of Mike's. I grab Bill's hoodie from the floor of the back seat where Trevor tossed it, and then I get out of the truck and start walking around to the back of the house to my entrance. I slide the key in the lock and notice that Trevor is behind me. "You didn't need to walk me to the door," I say without turning around. I push the door open and step inside, planning to turn and block Trevor's steps, but he pushes the door open more and steps inside. "Now what are you doing?" It feels like I've asked him this a million times tonight, but I can never figure out what's going on in his head. I cross my arms over my chest.

"What time are you seeing Bill tomorrow?" he asks, ignoring my question yet again.

"I don't know; probably like eleven."

"I'll be here at ten-thirty; we'll go talk to him before we go see July."

"How about I meet you at November's house at twelve?"

"I'll see you at ten-thirty," he says, grabbing the front of his hoodie I'm still wearing in his fist. My hands go to his biceps; holding on, I go up on my tiptoes. His mouth hovers over mine. I can feel his breath against my lips. "Are you going to be ready to go?" he asks, and I'm in Trevor's universe, so all I can do is nod my head. "Good. I'll see you then, baby." He says softly, right before his lips touch mine in a gentle, sweet kiss. He lets go of the hoodie, puts his hand on my belly, pushing me back from the door, then he's gone, leaving me standing there shocked and confused.

I go through my nightly routine on autopilot. My brain is mush from the emotional rollercoaster Trevor has put me on. I shake my head, toss Bill's sweatshirt onto the couch in the living room, walk down the hall towards my room, get undressed, go to the bathroom, wash off my makeup, and brush out my hair. I walk back to the bedroom and look around to make sure I'm still alone. After pulling Trevor's hoodie back on, I climb into bed and go to sleep, smiling because he's never getting his hoodie back.

A loud buzzing has me jumping out of bed. I look around, trying to figure out where it's coming from. I stumble and almost fall on my face when I see the time. "Crap," I moan, as I stumble to the door, stubbing my toe on the way. When I get there, I pull the door open, hopping on one foot while my other foot is in my hand, and see his gorgeous face smirking at me. I want to hit him, but instead I say, "I overslept," and start hopping down the hall towards the bedroom. I shut the door behind me, go into the bathroom, and pull off his sweatshirt, hoping that he didn't notice. Jumping into the shower, I wash off, and quickly get out. I wrap a towel around myself, then open the door and stop dead in my tracks when I see Trevor sitting on my bed. His back is against the headboard, and he's looking at a fashion magazine that I had on my nightstand. His legs are covered in black, baggy sweats; his plain white shirt is tight, and I can see the outline of his pectoral muscles. He has a tribal sleeve tattooed on one arm that travels up over his shoulder, and down one side of his body. I've never seen where it goes once it enters his pants, but I know how the top looks and tastes on his chest and arm. "Can you wait in the living room?" I ask. His head comes up; his eyes hit me and do a full body sweep, leaving me feeling naked—or more naked than I already am.

"If you kiss me."

"I'm not kissing you. I think it would be better if we never kiss again," I tell him, walking to my dresser to find a pair of lace boy shorts. I pull them on under the towel I'm wrapped in. I turn around, raising my eyebrows. "Can you wait in the living room?" I ask again, this time a little more annoyed, but he hasn't moved at all.

"Come kiss me and I'll wait in the living room."

My eyes narrow. "Is this like your newest game?" I ask on a head tilt. "I have to tell you, I'm not interested in playing with you, Trevor."

"No game," he says, shrugging. "Like I said before, we're going to be best friends."

I cross my arms over my chest. "I don't kiss my friends, so if you could kindly leave and let me get dressed, that would be great."

"We're going to do a lot more than kiss, baby," he says, smirking. I want to throttle him; instead, I grab a lace bra, a white tank top, and a pair of sweats. If he's going casual, so am I. Once I have everything I need, I head to the bathroom, leaving a smug looking Trevor on my bed. I slam the bathroom door for good measure. "Are you always this cranky in the morning?" he yells. I ignore him and get dressed.

Standing in front of the mirror, I wonder why he's acting so strange. I look to the ceiling, hoping for the answer. When we were friends before, he never kissed me; he never even hugged me until the night July was born. And our make out—and my almost-orgasm—night was more the vodka than anything else, so that doesn't even really count. "Why is he interested now?" I whisper, looking at myself in the mirror. I haven't changed. I pull my hair up into a messy bun on top of my head, do a couple swipes of mascara and a little blush, then I open the bathroom door. I look at the bed and see that Trevor is now laying down, with one arm thrown over his eyes, and the other against his abs.

"Trevor, let's go," I say, walking to my closet to grab a pair of sneakers. I sit in the chair next to the bed, bend and put them on, and he still hasn't moved. "Trevor," I sigh, going to stand next to him. I touch his arm lying across his stomach, tracing the tattoo that travels down his wrist. All the air is pushed out of my lungs when I'm grabbed suddenly, and tossed onto the bed with Trevor half on top of me. "What are you doing?" I breathe, trying to push him off.

"You haven't kissed me since I got here," he says, his hand going to the hair at the side of my head, sweeping it back.

"I'm not kissing you." I push him again and he doesn't budge.

"Did you sleep in my hoodie?" he asks. I completely freeze, trying to think of an excuse for wearing his hoodie. His face bends towards mine, his nose running along my jaw. I can feel him inhale, and somewhere in the back of my mind I wonder if he just sniffed me. "Did you sleep in it?" he asks again, this time quietly. I can feel goose bumps breaking out across my skin. His hand travels from my hip and down my thigh, to the underside of my knee. My brain is in overdrive, and the words that I want to say seem to have gotten stuck in my throat. "Did you wear something under it?" he asks, running his nose down my neck. "Or did you want to feel me wrapped around you all night?"

"We need to go." I say quietly, finally getting my brain to function. I push him again, and he presses me deeper into the bed.

"What scent is that?" He runs his nose along my jaw, behind my ear, and down my neck.

"Heaven," I gulp, as his hand behind my knee travels up to my hip again.

Softly, he whispers in my ear, "Yeah." He breathes against my skin, causing my heart to skip and my belly to drop. "That smell makes me want to eat you," he says, nipping my neck. *Oh God!* My thighs squeeze together automatically. *Oh my God!* My brain is screaming at me to stop this, but my hands itch to grab his head and drag his mouth to mine.

"W-we ne-need to go," I stutter out on a shaky breath.

"In a minute," he mumbles, right before his tongue touches the base of my neck, then it travels up to my chin. When his mouth crashes into mine, all thoughts leave my head. One of my hands goes to his bicep, the other to his head, running my fingers up the back of his scalp, pulling him closer. His mouth travels down my neck; the roughness of the scruff on his face rubs against my skin and all I can feel is fire, the same fire I felt the last time we were together. That thought is all I needed to snap out of this crazy moment.

"Trevor," I whisper, wishing that my voice would come out stronger. His eyes meet mine; they're darker than normal. He rubs his chin against mine; I bite my lip against the urge to moan or press into him. I want to scream. When we were friends, I told him things that I had never told anyone else. I trusted him. I had been falling in love with the person that he is, not the guy that every woman in town wants a piece of, but the real him. The one who listened to me when I shared the hurt of my past and the one who helps old ladies carry groceries across the street. The one who stopped in the middle of the road when he saw a bird with a broken wing, and the one who loves his mom so much, that no matter who's around or where they are, he hugs her and tells her he loves her. That guy; *that* was the Trevor that I was falling in love with. Then he showed me a side of him that was ugly and hurtful, a side that I can't forget no matter how much I want to.

"Are you okay?" he asks, and I nod my head, pushing against him.

"We need to go," I repeat for what feels like the millionth time.

"What's wrong?" he asks, and I almost want to laugh.

"I don't even know where to start," I shake my head. He pushes off the bed, pulling me up so that I'm standing in front of him. "I'm just going to be honest so that things don't end up crazier than they already are," I tell him, taking a step back. "First, thank you for the ride home last night." I look up into his amazing brown eyes and get lost for a second. He's so handsome; part of me wants to just say, "Screw it; Que Sera, Sera", throw caution to the wind, and get lost in bed with him for a day. But I can't do it; that's not me. I would end up crying or confessing my feelings for him, and he would walk away with another notch on his belt, while leaving me feeling alone and empty. "I'm going with you today to see July, but after that, I think that it would be best if we went back to the way things were. I'm not having sex with you. Just because I'm not a virgin doesn't mean that I'm going to sleep with you." I say in my most serious voice.

"You were going to sleep with me."

"Yeah," I whisper, feeling tears clog my throat. "Thankfully, that didn't happen. I mean, how humiliating would it be to have slept with you, then have you walk away without ever talking to me again," I laugh, but it's humorless and full of hurt.

"Listen, I was fucked up, okay? You're so innocent; I thought I was doing the right thing."

"So now that you know that I've had sex, you think it's okay to sleep with me?" I'm so confused by his logic.

"Stop fucking saying that you've had sex," he growls, his hands sliding down his face. "Jesus, I don't want to fucking talk or hear about that shit."

"Okay," I whisper, startled by the pissed off look on his face.

"I said I was sorry for that shit." I try to think back, but I'm pretty sure that he never apologized. "It's in the past; we're moving on and going to be best friends." I shake my head, wondering what it must be like to live in his universe. And why the hell does he keep saying that we're going to be best friends? I was starting to feel like I was in a bad episode of Barney. "We need to go," he says, walking out of the bedroom. I follow him out and watch as he bends to put on his shoes. He grabs his keys off the counter, I grab my bag, but when we get to the door, he stops and turns to me. "This is going to happen."

"What?" I ask, my eyebrows drawn together in confusion. His finger comes up and skims down the center of my face, forehead to chin.

"You and I, we're going to happen." He kisses me, then opens the door, putting his hand on the small of my back to lead me out. "We can get your bag later."

"I have my bag." I lift my hand, showing him my bag that's hard to miss since its hot pink and covered in glitter.

"Your overnight bag, baby." He puts his arm around my shoulders, pulling me into him.

"I'm not staying overnight with you, so I don't need an overnight bag," I say, as he helps me into his truck. He has to lift me into it because it's so tall, and there are no sideboards to step onto.

"You are," is all he says, slamming the door and walking around the back of the truck. He slides behind the steering wheel, looking over at me. "So where does the douche live?" I give him directions, and then we're on our way.

Chapter 3

Trevor

    I wake up feeling Liz's body pressed against mine. Her small hand is tucked under her cheek against my chest; her thigh is over my hip, and my hand is full of her pink lace-covered ass. Yesterday, after she gave me directions to douchebag Bill's house, and made me promise not to call him douchebag Bill to his face, we drove the thirty minutes a few towns over to his house. He lived in a newer neighborhood; the houses all looked the same. They call it "cookie cutter"; I call it lame. "This peach house is his?" I asked, looking over at Liz. "What the fuck is wrong with this guy?"

"Trevor, please be nice, okay? He's helping me find my brother."

"You want me to be nice? There's a fucking Mini Cooper in the driveway, a *yellow* Mini Cooper, Liz. What man drives that kind of fucking car? Jesus," I said, shaking my head and looking back at his house.

"Please," she whispered, her soft, sweet voice pulling at my heart. Looking into her beautiful eyes, I saw fear of rejection; she was still guarded. I fucked up with her. I didn't want to do that again; I needed her to trust me so we could move forward. I had been a coward, didn't want to admit what I was feeling for her, so I took the easy way out, found something that I thought I didn't like and latched onto it with both hands. Now, every time she said she wasn't a virgin, I wanted to rip someone's head off. No one should touch her but me, and from now on, no one would.

"I won't call him a douchebag to his face," I told her softly.

"Thanks," she said quietly, leaning across the seat to kiss my cheek. Something about that small act gave me hope. When we got out of the car, the front door opened, and Bill walked out wearing a pink polo and plaid shorts. I looked at Liz to see her looking at me, her eyes telling me to remember my promise.

"You didn't call me last night," Bill said, walking towards Liz, his face red.

"Sorry. I got home and went to sleep." She held out his hoodie towards him.

"You went to sleep?" His voice was sarcastic as he looked at her, then at me. "So you're telling me that *Trevor Mayson* drove you home and you went to sleep?"

"That's what I said, Bill." With her hands on her hips, she looked at me when I took a step forward. "I just want to know what you found out about my brother," she sighed in frustration. I knew she was upset, so I stepped towards her, pulling her into my side. Her body stiffened until I rubbed the smooth skin of her arm, listened as she let out a deep breath, and her body melted into mine. I couldn't help but to kiss the top of her head in approval.

"So you're with him now?" Douche asked, and I give him a smug look; my way of telling him to "suck it, she's mine".

"Yes!" I growled, at the same time she answered, "We're friends, Bill."

"Best friends," I said. She glared at me and I shrugged.

"Is this a fucking joke? I don't even live in your town and I know about the Mayson brothers."

"If you think he's going to be faithful, y—" He didn't get a chance to finish because I took a step towards him. He was starting to piss me the fuck off, and it was taking everything in me not to lay him out on his own driveway.

"I came here to bring you this." She shoved his hoodie at him while coming to stand in front of me. "I just want to know what you found out about Tim." I could hear the shakiness in her voice and knew she was on the edge. This shit with her brother was completely fucked up.

"I don't have any new information," Bill said.

"You told me last night that you had a new lead."

"I don't."

"If this is about Trevor—" she started, but he interrupted her.

"It's not about him; it's about you being a tease."

"I'm not a tease," she hissed, taking a step towards him. I pulled her back by her sweats before she could get too far. She looked up at me with murder in her eyes. I had the urge to kiss the fuck out of her, but I didn't think she would appreciate it very much at that moment.

"I told you he was a douche," I said on a shrug.

"Fuck you!" Bill said to me, and I laughed; this guy was a joke.

"Let's go, baby," I pulled on Liz's sweats, causing her to step back.

"Pussy," Bill said low. I pulled Liz behind me; I was about five inches taller than him; I bent down so my face was in his.

"Listen here, you little bitch! I'm being nice, but you keep pushing me and I will be forced to teach you some fucking manners. Don't play with me; I guarantee that you will lose." I bent deeper so only he could hear me, "Stay the fuck away from Liz; no phone calls, no texts, no visits. I hear you've made contact, you won't like what happens." I stood and patted Bill's chest. "Good talk," I said. Turning around, I pulled Liz with me and opened the door to my truck, lifted her, and sat her inside. I gave her a soft kiss on her forehead. Walking around to the driver's side, I slid behind the wheel, leaving douchebag Bill stunned and standing in his driveway, clutching his hoodie to his chest.

"Sorry," Liz whispered. I looked over to her; her forehead was resting against the window. I reached up, running my fingers down her arm. She had no idea how sweet she was; it made me want to lock her away so the fucked-up world didn't have a chance to contaminate her. It was hard to believe that she hadn't become jaded by the way people treated her when she was younger, or the way some still treated her. She's honestly one of the strongest people I know. Nico showed me a yearbook picture of her in high school; even with short hair and bad clothes, she was still pretty. She just looked run down, like she was fighting against the world. But looking at her in the truck, I couldn't help but appreciate her beauty, not only on the outside, but inside too.

"How 'bout we stop for coffee before we head out to see July?"

"Sure," she shrugged, keeping her head to the glass.

"How 'bout a cinnamon roll with that coffee?"

"Sure." She still didn't make a move to lift her head.

"How 'bout a quickie in the bathroom while we wait for our coffee and cinnamon roll?" Her head finally turned and she glared at me.

"I'm not sleeping with you." She crossed her arms over her chest with a pout, but not before I saw a small smile.

"Yet," I said, and she giggled. I don't think I had ever heard her giggle before; my stomach muscles tightened at the sound. Being around her, I had a permanent semi, but her giggle, and knowing that she wore my hoodie to bed, then seeing her in nothing but a towel with water still beaded on her skin, made me want to lick every inch of her. She had me with the worst case of blue balls ever; even when I was younger, it wasn't this bad.

"You're relentless," she said quietly, but she didn't make it sound like a bad thing.

"Hey," Asher said, answering the door. He didn't have a shirt on and I looked over at Liz to see if she was checking him out, but she only had eyes for July, who was also shirtless against his chest.

"Can I?" she asked, finally looking at my brother. I could tell that he didn't want to hand her over, but relented. I'm sure November told him that she would kick his ass if he didn't share.

"Hey, beautiful. You look more and more like your mamma," Liz whispered, kissing July's chubby cheek while walking into the living room. She sat on the couch; my heart squeezed at the sight of her holding my niece, her long blonde hair over the opposite shoulder that July's head was laid against. To see the comfort and ease she had with a baby was surprising.

Asher cleared his throat; I looked at him, brow raised. His eyes went to Liz, and then came back to me in a silent question. I shook my head.

"Where's November?" Liz asked, looking around.

"Taking a nap. July's been giving us a hard time; she doesn't want the bottle, so November's boobs are on tap, and it's wearing her out."

"Let me see a bottle," I said, walking over to Liz, sitting next to her.

"You wanna try feeding her?" Asher asked, walking into the kitchen to get a bottle out of the fridge.

"Let me see her, baby," I said quietly, next to Liz's ear. I could smell her subtle scent and my mouth watered, making me want to put my lips all over her. I could tell she didn't want to hand July over. When she finally gave in, I ran my fingers down her cheek to her chin, pulling her forward, trying not to scare her off. I kissed her softly on the edge of her mouth. I was glad I was not the only one affected. The small gasp she made let me know a lot more that she probably wanted me to.

"You need to stop kissing me," she whispered, looking away.

"Never," I told her, putting July in the crook of my arm. Asher walked back into the room holding a bottle.

"She won't take it. I can't even get her to drink it and I'm her favorite person in the world." Asher said, looking smug. I shook my head and chuckled.

I took the bottle from him, rubbing the bottle's nipple across her lips while squeezing it so some of the milk came out, and after a second, she latched on. She struggled a little, but I could tell she wasn't happy with the flow of milk, so I pulled it away when she started to fuss. I handed her to Liz, and headed to the kitchen so I could poke another hole in the nipple. When I was done, I took July back, and went through the same steps again. Once she latched on, I could see that she was content; I looked over at my brother, and he didn't look so smug anymore.

"Shit, bro. Why didn't I think of that? My poor wife has been exhausted, and I haven't been able to do a damn thing about it because she wouldn't take a bottle."

"What can I say? I know women," I shrugged. Asher looked over at Liz, who was watching July; he looked back at me and smirked. If I wasn't holding my niece, I would have punched him in the face. He thought this shit was funny. *Ahh, fuck, all my brothers did.*

"Sure, you do," he chuckled, walking to the kitchen to pull out some sandwich stuff from the fridge.

"Do you guys want to eat?"

"No, thanks," Liz said, her eyes never leaving July.

"Do you want kids?" I asked, her eyes meeting mine.

"No," she shook her head.

My heart froze. Looking at her, I could see the longing on her face with the way she looked at July. "Why don't you want kids?" I knew the question sounded almost angry, but she caught me off guard.

"I just don't," she whispered. Standing up, she walked towards the back door where Beast was sitting outside, looking in through the glass. She opened the door and stepped out. I watched as she walked down the back steps to the yard, picked up a ball, and threw it for him.

"What did you say?" Asher asked, coming back into the living room with a sandwich and chips. July finished eating, so I put her against my shoulder to burp. I looked back out the door and watched Beast run up to Liz with the ball in his mouth, his tail going a million miles a minute as she wrestled the ball from him, and tossed it again.

"I asked her if she wanted kids. When she said no, I asked her why not. She said she just didn't, and she got up and walked off."

"Dude, what the fuck?"

"What? It's just a question; she fucking shocked me saying that she doesn't want kids."

"Let's say she has a reason for not wanting a child. Do you think that she would tell you the reason? And why would she, when you're not someone she trusts?" He asked, shoving a huge bite of ham sandwich in his mouth.

I shook my head looking back out the window; she was now sitting on the grass, with Beast sitting on top of her. "I know it's fucked up, but she's it." He raised a brow at me. "I knew from the minute I saw her."

"She's your boom." He nodded in understanding.

"Yeah, but some shit went down, and I used it as an excuse to avoid what I was feeling and pushed her away. I was still trying to hold on, but it didn't work and blew up in my face. Now, I'm trying to figure out how the fuck to get back to where we were."

"The only advice I can give you is to stick with it, and it might not hurt to push her a little; it sounds like she's not going to be very open to a relationship with you. But don't give her a choice; play all your cards, even the ones that push her into a corner."

"Is that what you did, Don Juan?" I asked, looking down at July who had fallen asleep. If I got this in the end, I would do whatever was necessary.

"Fuck yeah!" he said, making me laugh. He shook his head, shoving chips into his mouth. "Laugh all you want, fucker, but look at my life. I have a beautiful woman wearing my ring in my bed every night, a little girl who couldn't be more perfect, and if God's feeling generous, I will have my wife knocked up before the years out."

"You trying for another already?" I asked, slightly surprised. July was just two-months-old and I figured they would wait a year.

"I need a son, dude. Fuck, my wife is beautiful, my daughter is going to be a knock out...I'm fucked unless I get another set of male eyes around here to help me out."

"You do know that shit's like fifty-fifty, right? You could end up with another girl."

"Naw," he shrugged, "I know it's going to be a boy this time." Shaking my head, I looked back out the window where Liz and Beast were laying down in the grass, her hand running over his head on her stomach.

I stood, taking July with me as I walked to the door, slid it open, and saw her head tilt back. "Come inside, baby; we need to go soon." She didn't say anything, but stood up, dusted her sweats and hands off while heading towards the house with Beast following behind her. She turned sideways to fit by me, and walked to the kitchen. She grabbed her bag off the counter, dug inside to pull out a box, and sat it on the counter while looking over at Asher.

"Can you give that to November for me?" Asher nodded, his mouth full of sandwich.

"What is it?" I asked, walking over to where she stood

"A pair of earrings that I know she will love," she said, running her finger down July's cheek. Her face changed so drastically that I couldn't breathe; she wanted this. I could feel she wanted a family, or at least a baby; the longing in her eyes couldn't be misinterpreted.

"Are you okay?" I asked. She startled, taking a step back.

"Yeah, just tired."

"You wanna take a nap?" I asked, handing July to her. She didn't answer, but her arms went around July, her head tilting down. "Do you?" I asked again, my lips going to her hairline, breathing in her scent. It was unusual, like musky vanilla; I wasn't lying when I said that her smell makes me want to eat her. That smell, that's all her, made my mouth water. Something about it made me hungry. I'd never been one for going down on a female, but I could see myself spending a lot of time consuming *her*.

"Yeah, I think I'll just go home after this."

"That's not what I meant."

"Trevor," she shook her head; Asher's advice came back to me.

"We're still going to dinner tonight. If you want, we can go to your house, pick up some clothes, go to mine, and take a nap for a couple hours before we need to get ready for dinner."

"I don't think we should have dinner," she whispered, looking over at Asher, who was sitting on the couch pretending not to listen.

"Too bad. Now, do you want to take a nap before, or not?"

"Geez, fine!" She glared, and I couldn't help but smirk. She was fucking cute as hell when pissed.

"Good. Kiss July and give her back to my brother," I said. Her lips thinned, but she listened; taking

July to Asher, she kissed her forehead, before handing her over to my brother. Then she walked back to the kitchen, grabbed her bag off the counter, swung it so it slammed into my stomach, and called goodbye to Asher as she walked out of the house.

"Jesus, you've got your work cut out for you, bro," Asher said, laughing. I had to agree, but knew that in the end, if I got my way, it would be worth it.

~~*

When Liz walked out of my bedroom in the dress she was wearing for dinner, I felt my zipper imprint on my dick. The floral sundress that hugged her body, showing off every single curve, made me want to drag the dress up her thighs and slide into her. The front was low, showing a fair amount of cleavage; the bottom reached just above the knee. On her feet were a pair of cream high heels that wrapped around her ankle, making me think of nothing but feeling them in my back as I plowed into her. Her hair was down and wavy, laying over the tops of her breasts. It didn't look like she had on a lot of makeup except for on her lips; they were shiny with pink gloss. "What the fuck?"

"What?" she startled, looking down at herself. I didn't even notice her looking at me while I was checking her out. I had on a pair of black jeans, a dark grey button-down shirt, and a black vest. This was me dressed up; I only wore a suit if forced, and there hadn't been too many occasions where that was necessary.

"You look beautiful."

"Oh, thanks." She smiled, her cheeks turning pink. "You look very nice yourself, Mr. Mayson."

I shook my head. "The only reason I'm going to look good tonight is because you're on my arm."

She smiled, shaking her head, "You really are good at that, aren't you?" She grabbed some stuff out of her purse and put them in a smaller bag.

"Good at what?"

"Making a woman feel like she's all you see."

"You *are* all I see." I told her truthfully.

"Whatever, can we just go?" Her eyes got wet, and my chest squeezed. I thought that we were making progress, but it seemed like we were stuck in limbo. I put my hands to her waist, lifted her onto the counter, stood between her legs, and fought the urge to look at where her dress had ridden up her thighs. "Now what are you doing?" she snapped, pushing against me. Taking her wrists, I held them behind her back.

"Baby, listen to me." Her breathing changed.

"I don't have a choice; you're a bully and bigger than me," she mumbled. She looked so cute that I leaned in and kissed her softly, before laying my forehead against hers.

"I know I fucked up, but I want you to give me a chance. If this doesn't work out, you don't ever have to see me again. But try for me."

I watched a tear slide down her cheek. I released her wrists, and holding her face, I slid the tear away with my thumb. "How do I know that you're serious about this?"

"Have you ever heard of me being in a relationship?" She shook her head in response.

"I haven't been in one. I never even thought about it until I saw you sitting on my parents' porch with your legs to your chest, a cup of coffee in your hand, your hair in a crazy mess around you. You looked beautiful; then you laughed and I knew that it was you for me. I wondered who you were, and when I found out that you lived in town and I had never even seen you before, I was shocked. So I started hanging out with you and found out that not only were you gorgeous, but also sweet. I didn't know what to do with how I was feeling about you, so I used the only thing I could to push you away. The problem was I didn't like it much when you gave me what I wanted." I brushed her hair back from her face; she still looked uncertain. So I walked over to the junk drawer and riffled through it until I found a pen and piece of paper. I wrote on it and handed it to her. She sat there, looking at it, and biting her lip. I handed her the pen; she took it, made a circle, and then handed the note and pen back to me.

Will you go out with me?

YES or NO

She circled yes. I smiled and she giggled, shaking her head. "You do know you're crazy, right?"

"I figure I missed out on this when I was young, so I should start now." She laughed, shaking her head again. I went back to her, and standing between her legs, I put my hands on her calves, running up her smooth silky skin to behind her knees. I pulled her deeper into me; I could feel the heat of her against me. Running my hands up her thighs, watching as they traveled up, then to her waist, I looked up to see her watching my hands too, while biting her lip. "You're going to have to be patient with me and grade me on a curve." I ran my thumbs on the underside of her jaw. "Can you do that?"

She swallowed. "As long as you don't hurt me again." I knew that until I fixed the trust I had torn apart with her, she would be on edge. But as long as she gave me the time, it was fixable.

"I can't promise that things will be perfect, but I can promise that I will do my best to keep you happy." I pulled back, kissing her forehead. "We need to get on the road so I can take you out on a date," I told her, pulling her off the counter.

"Alright, but I need to be home kind of early. It's my turn to open the store tomorrow."

"I told you, you're staying the night."

She laughed, patting my cheek. "Awww, Trevor. You have so much to learn about dating; you'll be lucky if you get to first base tonight." She stepped around me, grabbing her purse off the counter. "Are you ready?" she asked, tilting her head to the side. I was stuck in place.

"You're joking, right? I mean, you look like *that* and expect me only to kiss you?" She nodded. I know that I don't know much about dating, but seriously, what the fuck? Shaking my head, I walked to the back door and opened it for her to step out before me.

"I thought we were leaving?" She asked, probably confused that we weren't walking out the front.

"We are, but I'm not letting you climb in my truck wearing that dress. We'll take my car."

"You have a car?"

"Baby, there's a lot about me that you don't know," I told her, opening my garage. My black-on-black 1969 Chevy Nova was looking back at us. I drive my girl a few times a year; most people don't even know she exists.

"Wow!" Liz whispered, putting my hand on the small of her back. I led her to the passenger side, helping her inside. Once I had her buckled in, I went to the driver's side, sliding behind the wheel.

"You ready?" I looked over to where she was sitting; her fingers were running along the leather of the seat.

"Hmm?" she mumbled, her fingers running along the dash. I chuckled, watching her.

"You ready to go?" I asked again. This time, she startled, and her hand went to her lap.

"Oh yeah, sure," she mumbled.

"You like my car?"

"When I was in high school, I wanted to buy an old car and fix it up. My friend Cassy and I used to talk about doing it all the time."

"You know about cars?" I asked, surprised. My brothers and I are always doing something to our cars.

She started laughing, leaning her head back against the seat. The column of her throat was exposed, and my dick hardened while imagining her in that same passion underneath me, head thrown back, cheeks flushed, and eyes clouded with lust.

"I never said that," she laughed harder, shaking her head, taking me out of my thoughts. "I just wanted to do it. Good thing I couldn't afford to buy a car to fix up. God knows it would have ended up covered in house paint, and upholstered in old fabric with dogs or cats on it."

Laughing, I reached over and grabbed her hand, pulling it to my thigh. Her skin is so soft. "I'll tell you what." I take my eyes off the road for a second to look at her. "You stay the night with me, and I'll let you help me fix up a car."

"Will you let me choose any fabric I want?" she asked. I can hear the smile in her voice.

"Fuck, no!" I shook my head. I did not need to have a car upholstered in kitten fabric.

"Sorry, then I'm going to have to pass." She smiled, and I noticed she has two small dimples in the corners of her mouth. "So...you should call Nico and Cash and tell them that a girl at the bonfire is trying to get knocked up."

"What?" I asked, laughing.

"This girl at the bonfire was saying that she wanted to get knocked up by a Mayson. She didn't care which one, just as long as she ended up with one of you guys."

"What the fuck?" I yelled, causing Liz to jump.

"Sorry," she whispered. "I was going to call Cash this morning and tell him, but I forgot until right now." She said quietly, trying to tug her hand away, but I refused to let up.

"Jesus, some of the women in this town are so fucking whacked." I looked over and saw Liz biting her lip. I let go of her hand and pulled down on her chin. "Stop doing that, baby. Your lips are gonna be hurting too bad to kiss if you keep it up."

She took a breath. "Sorry about telling you like that; it just came out."

I shook my head. "Since Asher settled down, things have gone from bad to worse." It made me pissed to think of one of those bitches getting pregnant and one of my brothers being stuck with her. "Who was it?" I asked, grabbing her hand and putting it back on my thigh.

"Um...I don't know her name. She's really skinny and has long brown hair; she's cute. She was wearing jeans and a white tank top."

I nodded. I knew who she was talking about. "Jules. She has a thing for Cash, but he's not interested," I said, shaking my head. I pulled into the parking lot of the restaurant; it was a small steakhouse that was just outside of Nashville.

"Oh! I heard about this place. Old Mr. Deen said they have really great steaks here."

She started to get out, but I held her hand, mumbling a soft "wait for me." *Hey, I may not have had a girlfriend before, but I know what the fuck to do when you're dating. My mom would kick my ass if I treated any woman wrong.*

"Thanks," she said softly, pulling down her dress. I grabbed her hand when we got inside the restaurant. They sat us at a small table in the back near a large window with a view of the forest beyond. "This is really nice," she said, her eyes coming back to me. The waiter came over to take our order; we talked about town while we ate, we talked about her store Temptations, and I told her about the construction business and the new contract that we got. Everything with her was easy. I have never met a woman who I could laugh with and talk to about anything. I knew with her, her interest had nothing to do with money or my family name. I looked across the table, noticing her face has become red.

"You don't look too good, baby."

"I don't think you're supposed to say that out loud," Liz said from across the table, a small smile on her lips.

"No, baby. I mean, you look red and puffy; are you allergic to anything?"

"I never was before." She opened her bag, pulling out a small compact and held it in front of her face. "What the hell?" she mumbled, turning her face right, then left.

"Let's go. We can stop somewhere and get you some Benadryl; are you breathing okay?" I looked around for the waiter, trying to call him over.

"Yeah, but my mouth's starting to feel a little itchy." She laughed, "Don't even say anything,"

"I won't," I chuckled, finally catching the waiter's attention. He made his way over to us and I got my card back. Sliding it in my pocket and standing, I pulled out Liz's chair. Her face was now breaking out in hives and my concern was starting to grow, so I picked her up, carrying her bridal-style out of the restaurant. When we got to the front door, I hurried to my car. Liz tucked her face into my neck; I was sure she could feel that it was swollen. I kissed her hair and placed her in the passenger seat, making sure to buckle her in. "I'm gonna take you to the hospital."

"No, please, I just need some Benadryl and I'll be fine," she said on a wheeze, and I knew that she wasn't fine. I pressed the gas, and once I reached the emergency room entrance, I slammed the car in park, ran around to the passenger's side, and ignored the guy yelling not to park there. I pulled Liz into my arms. She passed out after two minutes in the car. I started running into the hospital; a nurse saw us and opened the door right away. I laid Liz on the bed, and then there was a ton of commotion around us.

I told them what she ate at dinner, and that she said she had never been allergic before. The doc gave her a shot and told me that it shouldn't take long for it to start working and for us to see some results. Looking down at her small body in that bed, my heart started beating out of my chest. I couldn't think of a time when I had been so fucking scared. I ran my hands over my hair and face. I kissed her forehead, holding her hand. I called her mom to tell her what was going on; she said she and George would drive back from Alabama tonight, but it would take a few hours for them to get into town. I called Mike to let him know that she wouldn't be home, in case he got concerned. I hadn't expected a lecture, or the safety of my balls being threatened. I sent my mom and brothers a text, letting them know what was going on. They all loved Liz and were worried;

I told them I had it and that there was nothing anyone could do. By the time I got off the phone, some of redness had reduced, and the swelling had gone down. I talked to the doctor about what happened; he said it could have been anything, but that she needed to be tested. He prescribed an Epipen, along with medication.

"Her breathing is now back to normal," the doctor said. "All her vitals are great. Now we just need her to wake up so she can sign some papers." I nodded, watching him walk off. I went to her bedside; running my hand down her face, pushing back her hair, her eyes started to flutter and I hold my breath. When I finally saw her beautiful green eyes, I let out the breath I was holding. "Hey, baby." I said softly, bending and putting my mouth to her forehead. "You scared the shit out of me."

"What happened?" she asked; I can hear the strain in her voice. I stood, reaching over for the pitcher of water next to the bed. I filled a cup, grabbed the straw, and held it for her while she took a sip.

"You had an allergic reaction to something you ate at dinner. The doctor said that you need to get tested to see what caused the reaction. He also prescribed you an Epipen so that if it happens again, you can take the shot right away."

"I've never been allergic to anything before." Her voice was quiet, tears started to fill her eyes.

"Hey, now, no crying. You're okay, I..." Jesus, I was going to say I love you, but I don't, do I? Shit, I do. I fucking love her. I swallowed, looking down at her; it was too soon. I knew that it would happen, but it was too soon; my stomach was in knots, and I felt sick.

"Are you okay?" Looking concerned, she lifted her hand to my cheek. I was not okay, but I would be. I shook my head, grabbed her hand from my face, brought it to my mouth, and kissed her palm.

"Just worried, baby. I'm going to go let the doctor know you're awake."

"Okay," she said quietly, laying her head back down on the pillow. After I found the doctor, he talked to Liz about seeing a specialist, and then went on to explain how to use the Epipen, and what she should do if something like this happened again. By the time we were pulling out of the hospital, it was after midnight. Liz was knocked out the minute I sat her in the car. Pulling up in front of my house, I carried Liz inside. She didn't even stir when I took off her dress and put one of my tees on her. I covered her up, and then went to check around the house to make sure all the doors and windows were locked. I took off my clothes, left on boxers that I normally would have forgone, and then climbed into bed, pulling Liz into me.

~~*

Bringing me back to the present, my fingers flex on Liz's ass in my hand. I look down at her; she's still sleeping, and I don't want to move, but need to get up and call my brothers to let them know that I'll be in late. My cell phone is in my jeans that I had on yesterday, and they're across the room on a chair. Like my thoughts make it happen, my phone starts ringing. Liz jolts, and then mumbles something, snuggling deeper into my side. I smile, slide out from under her, walk across the room, and grab my phone out of my pocket. "Shit," I whisper, looking at the screen. Mom is on the display. "One second, Mom," I whisper into the phone. I pull on a pair of sweats, holding the phone between my ear and shoulder. I look at the bed; Liz is still out, but now she's dragged my pillow to her front and is wrapped around it. I bend, kiss her hair, walk out of the room, and make my way down the hall into the kitchen. I bought my house two years ago. It was the only property I found with the acreage I wanted. I like the house; it's a fixer-upper with four bedrooms and 2500 sq. feet of ranch-style features. The kitchen is small, the living room is huge, the bedrooms are a good size, and it has a killer basement. Eventually, I'm going to tear down the kitchen's wall and make it an open-concept floor plan. But I'm taking my time, doing little-by-little. "Hey, Mom," I say into the phone, pulling out stuff to make coffee.

"Hey, honey. How's Liz? Did she get home okay yesterday?"

"She's still with me, Mom."

"She's still with you? It's seven-thirty in the morning." If it wasn't for the concern in her voice, I would have laughed. "What's going on, Trevor Mayson? So help me—if you hurt that girl..."

"Jesus, Mom, we're dating. I took her to the hospital last night. I didn't want her out of my sight, so I brought her here rather than digging through her shit to find her keys to stay at her place."

"Oh...okay," she pauses, probably stunned that Liz and me are together.

"Thanks for letting me know where your loyalties lie, Mom."

"Oh, stop. She's a good girl." I know my mom is rolling her eyes; we have always been close. I see movement out of the corner of my eye. I turn my head to see Liz standing in the doorway. Her hair is all over the place; my shirt is too big for her— about the same length as her dress from last night—and she looks adorable.

"Hey, baby. How are you feeling?" She shrugs, looking at the coffee pot. I can tell she's still half-asleep. "Come here." I say softly, holding up my arm. She stumbles to me, rubbing her face into my chest, and I kiss her hair. "Did you sleep okay?" I ask quietly, and she nods her head. Then I hear my mom sob into the phone. "Mom, you okay?"

"Perfect." She pauses a second. "Great, I'll let you go and call your brothers to tell them you're going to be late to the site."

"Yeah, alright."

"I'm happy for you, honey." She says quickly before hanging up. I sigh, tossing my phone on the counter. Mom's going to be flipping out. I lift Liz's face, checking her over. There is no swelling or redness; she looks much better, but not knowing what her reaction was from still worries me.

"You look a lot better."

"Why am I here?" she asks, then bites her lip like she didn't mean to ask.

I want to say, "Because this is where you will be from now on." But I know better. Plus, right now, she has her body pressed against mine, and I didn't even have to corner her. "You were really sick last night. I didn't want you to be alone."

"Oh," she mumbles. I smile, bending my head to touch my mouth to hers. When I pull away, her eyes slowly open. I love that look.

I pull her closer; both my hands go to her lower back above her ass. I pull up my tee. She shivers as my fingers run along her smooth skin. "You need to call the specialist and set up an appointment for as soon as possible while I make us something to eat," I say. Her eyes narrow, then she scrunches her nose up, shaking her head.

"It's too early for you to start being bossy." I smirk, pulling her closer and noticing her breath smells like mint.

"Did you brush your teeth?"

"I found a spare toothbrush in your cabinet and used it. I hope that's ok. I mean, you had like a hundred, so I didn't think you would notice." She smirks, and my gut clenches.

"My friend Frank is a dentist."

"Uh-huh." She shrugs, her eyes going over my shoulder to the coffee pot. She's thinking I'm full of shit and that when a chick stays over, I offer them a toothbrush in the morning, but it's not why I have them. I might be a dick, but I don't lie.

"Look at me," I say softly, pulling her attention away from the coffee pot. "You know my history, baby; it's not some big secret." Using her panties, I pull her deeper into me so she's forced to stand on her tiptoes. "But just like when I was honest with you about what I wanted, I was honest with them." I take a breath, kissing her softly. "I need to know now if you can handle that part of me." I need her to understand that I'm serious; this won't work if she second-guesses me. "I'm not going to be with you and feel like I need to tread carefully just because I have a past."

She's just staring at me, not saying anything. This goes on for a while. Finally, she says what I need to hear. "You're right. I'm sorry; I can handle it. Just promise that you will always be honest with me."

"Promise," I say against her mouth, sliding my hands down the inside of her panties. Pulling her up, her legs go around my waist. Her breathing picks up as I set her on the counter; my mouth is on hers, tasting, licking, and biting. When she moans, I start to pull back, kissing her more softly, not wanting it to get out of hand when I don't have time to thoroughly appreciate her. "Go get your phone while I fix us something to eat," I tell her, running my hands along the smooth skin of her thighs. I'm torturing myself; I need to either go take care of myself, or take a cold shower.

"Fine," she pouts, jumping off the counter. I grab her and give her a quick kiss, then go about fixing us breakfast.

Chapter 4

Liz

"Oh, honey! I'm so glad you're okay," Mom says as soon as I walk into the store. I'm not sure I am okay; I feel like I'm living in an alternate universe. I'm now girlfriend to the notorious player Trevor

Mayson; then this morning, before we left his house, he told me that he would be picking me up and we were, and I quote, "Going to pick out a puppy." I don't even have my own place. I still need to look for an apartment, and even in an apartment, I don't need a dog; so I told him that, and he said, "We're getting a dog; it's what couples do." I shook my head, trying to remember that he had never had a relationship before, so he didn't know that people who just started dating didn't buy living things together. They didn't even buy an inanimate object together. My case was lost when his mouth crashed into mine and I forgot what we were arguing about.

"I'm fine, Mom. I made an appointment this morning with a specialist to get tested." I hear laughing and turn around to see Britney and Lisa standing near the rack of scarfs. I'm sure that there will be rumors of me having some crazy disease running rampant around town by tomorrow. I look at my mom to see her watching the girls through narrow eyes. I'm not even bothered by them anymore; they're bullies and have nothing better to do with their time. I start walking to the back of the store, when the bell over the door rings. I turn to see Trevor, Cash, and Nico walk in.

"Hey, baby," Trevor says.

"Yo," Cash says, giving me his carefree smile.

Nico walks in, giving me a chin lift.

Cash and Nico walk over towards Britney and Lisa; Trevor comes right to me, his hand to my waist, pulling me a step closer. He bends, touching his mouth to mine. I automatically kiss him back, and when my eyes open, he's smiling down at me like always. "What are you doing here?"

"We wanted to get something for Ma for her birthday, so we came here to see if you could help us out."

"Oh, yeah. Sure, just give me a minute. I need to put my stuff down," I tell him, trying to pull away. But his fingers have hooked on the inside of my jeans, holding me in place.

"How are you feeling?" he asks, and my heart melts into a giant puddle right there in the middle of Temptations.

"Perfect." I say quietly, watching his face go soft. I love that he cares enough to worry about me. I turn my head; my mom is watching us, smiling like the cat that got the cream. I roll my eyes at her.

"So, Trevor," my mom says, pushing her way between us. "I know its short notice for booking a flight, but if you can get time off, would you want to go to Jamaica for my wedding? I'm sure you could room with Liz." She smiles, looking between us like she just solved world hunger with her suggestion.

"Mom, I'm sure he has better things to do." I'm still trying to get used to the knowledge that he's my boyfriend. Going to a foreign country with the guy you're dating is right up there with picking out a puppy; you should be together a while for both. Although, the thought of watching Trevor on a beach in nothing but a pair of board shorts over a long weekend sounds like a good idea.

"Sure, I can make it," he says. I look at my mom; she's looking at Trevor. I blink a few times, trying to clear my head.

"You don't have to come. I'm sure that you have a lot going on with the contract you just got," I tell him.

"I have three brothers. It's only three days; they can handle it."

"Oh," I say, wondering how the hell this is my life, and when I got sucked into Trevor's universe.

"Tonight, after we pick our puppy, we can try to get me on the same flight as you. If they don't have any seats left, you can change your flight to whatever one I'm on."

"You're getting a puppy?" my mom cries, clapping her hands.

"Someone kill me," I mumble, looking at the ceiling.

"What honey?"

"Nothing...I'm going to put my stuff down, then help the guys pick out something for Mrs. Mayson."

"I'll help them while you get settled," my mom says, putting her fingers around Trevor's bicep. I watch her give it a squeeze, then she looks up at him smiling. "Oh my, so strong. Do you work out?" Oh my God, someone? Anyone? Save me! Trevor smiles down at my mom, answering her in the affirmative. I walk into the back room and put my stuff away. I take a minute to bang my head against the wall a few times before I walk back out into the insanity that has become my life. It's after the guys left the store, and after my mom came back from her Trevor high, that I get a text from my brother.

Tim: Call me at this number 521-649-4579

I look to make sure my mom is still at the front of the store. "Mom, I'm going to be in the back."

"Sure, honey." She motions me away with a wave of her hand. I walk to the back of the store, sit down on a large box, and take a deep breath before dialing the number that he texted me.

"Liz, I need your help," I hear Tim say through the fuzzy connection.

"You want my help, after you stole from me and Mom? Are you high?" I ask, my voice becoming louder. I stand and peek out the door to make sure my mom didn't hear anything. Thankfully, she's still standing behind the cash register.

"I didn't want to do it."

"Where is the money, Tim?"

"Listen to me," he yells. I have never heard my brother yell before; my mouth snaps shut and my eyes close, knowing that whatever is going on is bad. Really bad.

"I know I fucked up, sis." He doesn't say anything else, so I take the phone away from my ear to make sure the call didn't drop.

"Tim?"

After a few more seconds, he finally speaks, sounding completely defeated. "I have a problem, and I thought that if I could just pay off the people I owed, that I could make a clean start."

"No," I whisper, my head falling forward.

"I never wanted this to happen, sis. You have to believe me. I was so depressed, and it was the only thing that could make me forget. Every time I made a bet, I thought, 'This is it. This is the last time...'"

"So you don't have a drug problem? You're addicted to gambling?" I want to make sure I'm hearing him right.

"Yes," he says softly.

"Why didn't you talk to me or Mom?"

"What was I supposed to say? I have a gambling problem, and I need money to pay off a loan shark that I stole from?"

"You could have started with that."

"Are you listening to me at all?"

"Yes!" I yell into the phone. "I'm listening to you. I almost lost my business; I *did* lose my apartment. I had to get a job at a strip club to try and come up with the money that was due on my business loan."

"You work at a strip club?" I could hear the anger in his voice.

"I did, until Trevor made me quit, and Mike gave me the money to pay my bills."

"Mike let you work for him?"

"Are you listening to yourself right now, Tim? You have no right to be mad. I had to work there because of you."

"I know. But Jesus, Liz, what the fuck?"

"Don't worry about it. I'm not working there anymore. Tim, Mike gave me that money, so you're going to have to find a way to pay him back. You need to come home."

"I can't come home right now."

"Why not?"

"I told you that I was going to pay the guy off that I borrowed from. Well, I did, but he wants interest on the money. I can't come home until I find a way to get it for him."

"Tim, stop being stupid and come home. Get a job; maybe you can work for Mike."

"I don't want to bring the shit that's following me to town, Sis."

"How much money is it that you owe?" I ask, doing calculations in my head, trying to think of what I might have to give.

"Ten G's."

"What the fuck, Tim?" I yell, and then cover my mouth. "You stole over twenty from me. Did you give it all to him, or did you snort it or shoot it up? I mean, that's a lot of money."

"I know. That's why I was calling. I wanted to see if you could loan me the money. I would pay him off, then come home."

"Tim, I'm not going to send you that kind of money. I don't even have that kind of money. Just come home and we can figure something out. We can, I just don't know what will work. I'll talk to Trevor," I say, wondering if I really would talk to Trevor. He is already pissed at my brother; this would only add to his list of reasons to dislike him.

"What the fuck does Trevor Mayson have to do with this shit?"

"We're dating, and he has a construction company. Maybe you could work for him."

"You're dating Trevor Mayson? Are you fucking stupid?"

"You owe a loan shark lots of money; are *you* fucking stupid?" Crap. I didn't mean to say that. I close my eyes, taking a breath. "Look, I like him, and we're seeing each other."

"I'm going to see if I can make it to town. I'll talk to Mike and see if I can work something out with him."

"You need to fix this," I whisper, tears clouding my eyes.

"I haven't gambled in a few days, okay?" Is that what all addicts say so they can avoid talking about their problems?

"Where are you now?"

"I'm with a friend. I'm sorry, Sis. I never meant for this to happen."

"Just come home, Tim. Mom's getting married in a few weeks; she's going to be expecting you to walk her down the aisle."

"I'll see what I can do."

"Please, come home," I whisper into dead air. I pull the phone away from my ear, knowing he hung up. I send a silent prayer up to whoever is listening, wipe the tears from my eyes, and start cleaning up the stock room.

~~*

"What about that one?" Trevor asks, pointing at a small, fluffy, white dog. I know most girls would go gaga over the small little ball of fur, but to me, he looks like he could get lost easily in my messy room.

"I don't know," I say, looking up at Trevor. His hand comes to the back of my head, twisting in my hair; my lips part right before he kisses me. "What was that for?" I breathe, when his mouth leaves mine.

"You look adorable right now," he smiles, pulling me under his arm, walking us down the long row of dog cages. We drove to the nearest ASPCA after he told me that I didn't have a choice, and that we were going to pick out a dog whether I liked it or not. So I told him that the only way we were getting a dog was if we adopted one that needed a home. "What about him?" he asks, stopping in front of a cage with a dog that could fit in my pocket and should be on a Taco Bell commercial.

"Um..." I bite my lip and look up at him again. "Do you like small dogs or something?" Every dog he's stopped to look at has been small.

He shrugs, looking around. "No, I just thought that girls liked small dogs."

"Trevor, I don't need a dog right now. I need to find another apartment; even then, I don't know if `I will be allowed to have a dog."

"First of all, it will be our dog; second of all, you don't need to find an apartment; you're staying at Mike's until you're ready to move in with me." All the air in my lungs pushes out. I look at Trevor and he is looking around like he didn't just tell me that we were going to be living together. Instead, he looks like he just told me what kind of coffee he prefers. "What about him?" he asks, dragging me behind him. My legs are like jelly; I still haven't taken a breath. I feel lightheaded. When did this relationship start moving at the speed of light? I stumble behind him, my legs taking a second to catch up with me. When we stop, I was looking the opposite direction of him. My eyes land on a giant black dog, and when our eyes meet, its head tilts to the side. I follow and do the same head tilt. We stare at each other for a few seconds before it puts one giant paw up on the door of its cage. I lift my hand, walking towards the dog. When it whines, I know it is the one. I hadn't even wanted a dog, but know that this guy, or girl, is mine.

"Hi," I say, walking over to the cage. On the door is some information about the animal. I see that it's a girl, and they don't know how old she is, just that someone found her on the side of the road and brought her in. The information packet explains that she's very friendly, and she seems to be house trained. I squat down in front of her, pressing my hand flat against the cage. Her paw comes up to my hand, and then her wet nose presses against my skin. I put my fingers through the chain link to give her a scratch. "You're a sweet girl, aren't you?" I look at Trevor, who has squatted next to me. He doesn't look too sure about her, but I am; if he doesn't want her, I'm going to call Mike and see if he will allow me to have a dog. I grab Trevor's hand and put it against the chain link; she smells him, then licks his palm. "She likes you."

"So she's the one, huh?" he asks, looking around at all the other cages. I start to do the same thing, when she whines, pawing the door of the cage. I laugh, sticking my fingers back through to her.

"She's perfect, don't you think?" His eyes meet mine, and there is such warmth there, that I hold my breath.

"Yeah, she's perfect." He leans forward to kiss me, and then pulls me up to stand with him. "What do you want to name her?" He looks at the card, and then back at me.

"Lolly?" I say, and she barks, making me laugh again.

"Well, let's go sign the paperwork so we can get Lolly home." We walk towards the front of the kennel, out the metal doors, and up towards reception.

"Did y'all see one ya liked?" the lady behind the counter asks, smiling. She has on a pair of bright blue scrubs with puppies playing soccer on them. Her nametag says her name is Mabel, and with her white hair pulled back in a loose bun, she looks like a typical southern grandma.

"The Rottweiler in cage seventeen," Trevor tells her.

"Aw, she's so sweet. I took her home with me last weekend and she was so good with my grandbabies! You two got any kids?" she asks, looking between us. I started to say no.

"Not yet," Trevor says, putting his arm around my waist, his thumb hooking on the inside of my jeans. I know I'm completely stiff; I don't want kids. I told Trevor that the other day when he asked me if I wanted children. Apparently, he only hears what he wants.

"You two will sure make some pretty babies." I can feel my hands start to sweat at her comment. I love kids, but every time I even think about having my own, I feel panicked. I'm not so delusional that I don't know exactly where my anxiety comes from. My dad died when I was young. I was abandoned, and don't want to have a kid and do the same thing to them. Will I get over it one day? I don't know; but right now, the thought of having children makes me feel nauseous.

I grab the paperwork from her and go to sit down in one of the chairs, trying to get my thoughts back under control. When Trevor comes over to sit down, he looks me over, then leans in like he's going to kiss me. I lean back; maybe it's petty, but he needs to hear me and what I'm saying, not whatever he has made up in his head. "I told you the other day that I don't want kids. That's not something that is going to change."

"So, never? You never want kids?" My heart breaks a little in that moment; the thought of never having a child makes me want to curl up and cry, but the thought of having one makes me feel sick.

"I don't know, to be honest with you." I look down at my hands, watching my knuckles turn white from squeezing the pen in my hand so tightly. "And I'm sorry; if that's a deal breaker, then we should just stop right now before feelings get involved." I look up into his eyes; they are warmly looking into mine, but they're also concerned. He leans forward, taking my hand and removing the pen.

"Aren't feelings already involved?" he asks, running his thumb over the back of my hand. I know mine are; I search his eyes, seeing my same feelings reflected back at me. He nods his head, then put his forehead to mine. "We're going to talk about this. Not right now, not tomorrow, but soon, and when we do, you're going to be honest with me. And then I'm going to set you straight by telling you that you not giving the gift of your love, kindness, and strength to a child of your own would be a tragedy." Wow. My breath catches, and I can feel my nose start to sting with tears. I can't believe that Trevor Mayson can be so sweet. He kisses my forehead, his lips lingering there. "Now, let's get this done so we can get our dog home."

"Okay," I whisper, wiping away a stray tear. We finish filling out the paperwork, which seems to take a lot longer than I expected; you would think that we are trying to apply to work for the Secret Service with the kind of questions they ask.

"So, do y'all want me to get some dog food for ya? At least enough to hold you over for tonight?" I look up at Trevor, realizing that I know nothing about having a dog. I hope he has more experience than I do with this.

"The pet store in town will still be open; so we'll just stop in there on our way home and get all of the supplies we need for her."

"Aw, see? Y'all are going to make great parents." She smiles, and my hands start to get sweaty again. "Let me just put y'all in the system, then I'll go get her for ya." She takes our paperwork and starts typing away on the computer; once she's done, she pulls a new leash out of a plastic bag, stands, and walks to the back room. My heartbeat picks up. I'm excited about this; at first, when Trevor said we were going to get a dog, I didn't know what to think. Now, knowing that Lolly was going to be going home with us, I was excited. When the door opens, Lolly sees us and starts barking.

"Well, are you ready to go home?" I ask her, patting my thighs and making her more excited.

"Here ya go, darlin'," Mabel says, handing over the leash. I feel like my face is going to split, I'm so happy. Trevor bends down, holding both sides of Lolly's face.

"Alright, girl, you ready to go?" Her front paws come off the ground, landing on his thighs, her tongue trying to reach his face. "I take that as a yes," he says with a grin, standing.

"If y'all have any questions, don't be afraid to call us," Mabel says, waving at us when we walk away. Once we get outside, Trevor lets down the gate of the truck.

"Is that safe?" I ask, not really feeling comfortable with Lolly riding in the open back of the truck where she can jump out.

Lolly jumps up like she has done it every day of her life. And who knows? She might have. Trevor slams the gate, walks to the passenger side, and opens the door for me to get in. Before I know what's happening, he has me by the waist, and is lifting me into the cab like I weigh nothing at all. Once I'm seated, he grabs the back of my neck, pulling my upper body forward so his mouth can reach mine. I love kissing him. He always has this taste, almost like cinnamon, but not as spicy. He smells that way too, along with something a little darker.

"Yum," I whisper, when his mouth leaves mine. He smiles, kissing me again; this time it's just a peck.

"Alright, baby, let's get to the store so I can get you girls home and find something to cook for dinner."

"Alrighty," I mumble, clicking my seatbelt in place. Once Trevor is behind the wheel, he starts up the truck and begins to back out of our parking space. He then stops, puts it in park, unclicks my seatbelt, grabs the waist of my jeans, pulls me into the middle of the cab of the truck, pulls the seatbelt around me, puts the truck back in reverse, and finishes backing us out of the space, and out the parking lot. "If it was bothering you so much, you could have asked me to sit in the middle, instead of manhandling me."

"I didn't know you sitting over there bothered me, until you were sitting over there," he says with a shrug. I shake my head, knowing there is no point in arguing. "What do you want for dinner?" This is such a normal question between people who are seeing each other, that I didn't know how to answer him. "We can pick something up, or when we get home, I can throw some steaks on the grill."

"Let's just pick something up."

"Sure," he replies, pulling me into his side. And that's when I know that we are really starting something beautiful.

~~*

"Please," I mumble. We have been doing this same thing every day for the last couple of weeks. I'm ready to kill Trevor; I'm not sure if there's such a thing as blue balls for women, but if it's possible, I have a horrible case of them.

"We have to stop, baby," he grumbles, rolling to his back, his arm going over his eyes. I can't take it anymore. I'm in actual pain; even though he has explained it more than once, I do not understand for one second why he keeps putting off us sleeping together. I roll out of bed, run to the bathroom, and slam the door. I feel bad; I know that every time he turns me down, he's hurting himself as well. It was endearing for the first week; now I'm starting to feel like he doesn't want me like I want him. How would any woman feel if the guy who is known around town for being a male slut-bag kept saying no every time her hands started moving towards his X-rated body parts? I turn on the shower and jump in before the water even gets hot; the freezing cold water beating down on me helps get my body back under control. "How much longer can I do this?" I whisper, leaning my head against the tile behind me.

Chapter 5

Trevor

"Jesus," I groan, shifting my dick to the side. Three weeks of having Liz in my bed every night without taking her is killing me. I want to build on our relationship before we add sex into the mix. Every woman I have ever been with was for one reason and one reason only, and I don't want that with her. But I can read the signs; she's becoming fed up with my do-not-pass-second-base, do-not-collect-the-pussy rule I have instigated. Every day it is becoming harder and harder not to slide into her, or put my mouth on her. Rolling out of bed, I pull up a pair of cut off sweats. I can hear the shower running; knowing she's in there wet and soapy makes it harder to leave the room. I walk down the hall to the kitchen, flip on the coffee pot, and Lolly comes in through the dog door I put in last night. She's wagging her tail and I bend over to give her a rub down. "You want breakfast?" I ask her, leaning over to open the cabinet to get out a can of wet food. I mix it with some dry food and set it on the floor in front of her. I hear my cell ring from my bedroom. I walk down the hall and over to what was now my side of the bed. Liz likes to sleep on the right side, not that it matters; we always end up in the middle.

"Yeah?"

"Yo, T. We gotta go to Alabama today to pick up an order."

"No, take Nico with you."

"He's up with Kenton in Nashville. It's just one night, T. Jesus, you already pussy whipped?"

If any of my brothers knew that I have been putting sleeping with Liz off, they would have a fucking heyday with that shit. "Its overnight?" We hadn't had an overnight trip in a long time, and the idea of sleeping without Liz doesn't sit well.

"We leave this afternoon from the site, and we should be back tomorrow night." Just then, the bathroom door opens. Liz steps out in nothing but a small towel that doesn't cover much.

"Yeah, alright. Make the reservations," I mumble into the phone, not taking my eyes off her.

"Sure. See you at the site. Say hi to Liz." He hangs up. I toss my phone on the bed and start stalking towards Liz, who now looks like she's stuck in place. I feel the smile hit my face, and her eyes narrow.

"Do not touch me, Trevor Mayson." She takes a step back when I lunge at her.

"I like touching you, and you like me touching you."

"No. No more touching," she moans, her body bowing back against my arm, trying to put space between us.

"I'm going to be gone overnight," I mumble, sliding the stubble of my chin along her neck. She moans, her body melting into me. I love that she responds so easily to my touch. I take her earlobe into my mouth, biting down gently. I'm so hard that the feel of my boxers against my erection is killing me. "You're going to sleep here tonight and keep my side of the bed warm. Right, baby?" I ask, my hand sliding down to the bottom of the towel, running my fingers along the edge. I don't know why I keep doing this to myself. I listen as her breathing changes; her breaths coming faster and faster as my fingers run up her thigh. "Are you listening to me?" I whisper, as I bite lightly down on her neck.

"What?" she moans, her fingernails scrapping against my scalp. She loves my hair. If it wasn't such a bitch to take care of, I would let it grow out so she could grab on to it when I'm eating her. "I'll stay at my place with Lolly."

"No, you'll stay here with Lolly. All her stuff is here; she's used to being here." I'm grasping at straws, but I like her here in my space, knowing that when I get home she will be waiting for me. I lick her mouth, her chin, her neck, her collarbone; her fingernails are digging into my scalp. All I want to do is toss her on the bed, spread her legs, and feast; or I'd pick her up, press her into the wall, and slide into her, but there is no time for either. We both have to get to work. My hands go to her face, holding her gently. "Just give me peace of mind and stay here."

"Fine!" she cries, trying to bend further away, but she's so tiny that I can pick her up with one hand if I want.

"Just put my mind at ease and stay here." I say quietly, distracted by the feel of the skin on her thighs.

"I said I'll stay here; so let me go so I can get ready for work." I squeeze her ass; she moans, still trying to pull away.

"You gotta know, it's killing me not to slide inside you." I press my erection into her belly; she bites her lip, shaking her head. "It is," I tell her, pressing her against the wall, determined to at least get her off before I have to be away overnight. Putting more pressure on her hips stills her movements. Sliding my hand from her ass to her belly, I look into her beautiful face. Her cheeks are flushed, her lips are swollen, and her unusual green eyes are dark with lust. "I'm going to make you come, baby." Biting her neck, my fingers slide through her wetness, making her hips jerk. She whimpers, holding onto my biceps, her sharp nails digging into my skin. My mouth lands on hers, doing to her mouth what I want to do to her pussy. I slide in one finger, then another, curving them up. Her head falls back against the wall. "Open your eyes." I can feel her getting closer; it takes everything I have not to drop to my knees, toss her leg over my shoulder, and take her with my mouth. When she looks at me, I use my thumb and press, then circle, her clit two times. She clamps down on my fingers, screaming my name, her head falling back, her eyes closing. When her eyes open, she gives me a smile I have never seen on her before. I want to take my fingers and suck them into my mouth, but my restraint is already slipping and knowing how she tastes would be the final straw. I pick her up, carrying her to the bed. I sit with her in my lap, her face going into the crook of my neck. I start to laugh at how relaxed she is.

"Are you laughing?" Her words mumbling into my skin make me laugh harder. Her face comes out of my neck and she glares at me. "What's so funny?"

"Now I know if you get in a huff, all I have to do is give you an orgasm, and you settle your ass down."

"You did not just say that." She shakes her head, but doesn't move from her spot on my lap. "So, you're going to be gone overnight?"

"Yeah, we need to go pick up an order." I pull her face away from my chest to look into her eyes. "The wedding's coming up," I remind her; I'm excited to spend the weekend on the beach with her half-naked.

"I know." Her voice cracks and I'm reminded of her shithead brother. She's worried that he won't be able to find the money to pay back the guys he owes.

"I'm going to call Kenton and see if he can track him down." I pull her tighter, rubbing circles on her back. We sit like that for a while, her body so relaxed that I think she's asleep. Its' crazy how much my life has changed, and how happy I am now that I have accepted what I was feeling for this beautiful woman who seemed so shy the first time I met her. Little did I know, she's not shy at all, just quiet; it's almost like she studies people before taking a chance and talking to them. "It's going to suck sleeping without you, even if you are a bed hog," I say, feeling her smile against my chest.

"How can I be a bed hog when you basically sleep on top of me?" True, I have never been one to cuddle; but with her, I like knowing where she is, and that she can't get away without me knowing. "I guess I should get up and get dressed. It's my turn to open the shop."

"Yeah, I need to pack and meet Cash at the site." Her lip pouts out, so I bite it, giving it a gentle tug. "Just think, in a few days, it will be you, me, ocean, sun, and sand."

"I know. I'm just worried about Tim. He called the other day saying that he didn't know if he was going to make it." She rolls her eyes.

"I told you how I feel; I think you need to let your mom know what's going on."

"I can't!" She jumps up so fast that she almost falls over. "Mom is stressed about the wedding; if I told her what was going on with Tim, she'd call it off to deal with his problems. She deserves her happily ever after."

I hold up my hands, warding her off. We have been through this a few times already, and every time, it comes back to the same thing. "If he shows up for the wedding, I'm kicking his ass."

"No, if he shows up for the wedding, *I'm* kicking his ass." I lean forward, grab her behind her thighs, and drag her forward to stand between my legs.

"Why don't you call November and see if she wants to do dinner tonight? I'm sure she wouldn't mind getting out of the house for a little while."

"I doubt that Asher will let her leave the house," she grumbles, looking adorable.

I laugh, pulling her closer. My brother loves his girls, but said the other day that November needed a break. And I'd feel better knowing that Liz had something to do while I was out of town.

"Just call her."

"Fine," she sighs. I know she misses her friend.

"You need another orgasm?" My hands slide up the back of her thighs.

"What? No!" she laughs, her cheeks turning pink while she tries to take a step back. So I hold her behind the knees tighter, pulling her even closer.

"You sure? You seem a little grumpy, baby."

Her eyes narrow, making her look cute as hell. "I need to get ready to work. And you need to pack."

Running my hands up the back of her thighs again, my fingers curve inward. "Kiss me and I'll let you go." Seeing the effect my touch has on her makes my blood pound. It is its own aphrodisiac; I love knowing that I was the one who made her lips swollen, eyes darken, and cheeks turn pink. I want to beat my chest like a fucking caveman. "Come on, kiss me," I say, squeezing her thighs tighter.

"Fine," she sighs, bending her face towards mine. I fist the hair at the back of her head, causing her to moan.

"You really want another orgasm, don't you?" I see her eyes flash right before I pull her mouth to mine, getting as much of her taste inside of me as I can.

~~*

"Holy shit!" Cash says.

"What?" I look over at him, expecting some kind of disaster to be happening in my truck. He's looking out the windshield. I follow his gaze and see a girl with shoulder–length, bright red hair, creamy skin, and a short summer dress holding the door open for a woman with a stroller.

"You know her?" I ask, looking back at him, noticing he looks a little star struck.

He looks over at me with his big cheesy smile. "Nah, but I will."

I chuckle and finish parking the truck. When we get out, the girl looks back; her face turns bright red when she realizes Cash is looking at her. Cash looks at me confused; I smirk and shrug my shoulders. She's definitely cute, but completely opposite of the forward women who normally don't even give my brother a chance to hit on them.

I poke him in the ribs with my elbow, bending close so only he can hear me, "Do you even know how to hit on a woman?"

His eyes narrow right before he smirks, stepping in front of me in line to stand next to her at the counter. "This should be good," I mumble to myself, listening to Cash tell the cashier that he and the girl are together so he can pay for her coffee.

"We're not together," the girl tells the cashier, who is staring at Cash.

"We are; I'm paying," Cash says, sliding the money to the cashier. When I look at the girl, I can tell she's getting annoyed when she blows the hair out of her face. They both take their coffees; she turns on Cash.

"Here." She shoves money at him, hitting him in the chest with it, catching him off guard, making him stumble back into me; his coffee goes all over the front of his shirt.

"Crap, I'm so sorry! I didn't mean for that to happen!" She starts pulling napkins out of the dispenser and pats Cash down. "Why couldn't you just let me pay for my own coffee?" she grumbles, not even looking up. Cash starts to laugh, and her head flies up, busting him in the chin. I can actually hear his teeth slam shut and the crack of his chin to her head. "This is so humiliating," she whispers; looking up, her hands go to her head, and tears form in her eyes.

"Let me see your head, honey," he says quietly, pulling her forward, taking the coffee out of her hand, and handing it to me. I watch him drag her to the side and talk quietly to her; when I hear her light giggle, I know they're both going to be okay. I feel my phone vibrate, and when I pull it out, I see that it's Jen calling. I don't know how many times I'll have to tell this chick that I'm not interested before she'll clue in.

"What, Jen?"

"I want to see you."

"I told you before; we're done."

"I...I miss you." This chick is completely whacked; my face tilts towards the ceiling, and I pray for patience.

"I'm only going to say this one more time: we were never anything, so stop fucking calling me." I hang up and see a text message from Liz.

> **Liz:** Missed you last night.

My heart flips over; I feel like a chick standing here smiling at my phone.

> **Me:** Miss you too baby.

I look around and see Cash watching me.

"What's that smile for?" he asks, taking the girl's coffee from my hand and handing it back to her. I look at him, and his smile matches mine. I look at the girl and see her blush when he hands her the coffee.

"Nothing. Liz messaged me," I tell him, walking up to the cashier to order my coffee.

"This is Lilly. Lilly, this is one of my brothers, Trevor," Cash introduces.

"Nice to meet you."

"Hi," she says shyly. "Um, I need to go; it was nice meeting you both. Again, I'm really sorry about the coffee...and the head-butt."

I chuckle, and Cash laughs. "Its fine, honey. I'll walk you out," he tells her. I get my order, and order another coffee for Cash, before I head out of the coffee shop. When I step out, Cash and Lilly are talking quietly off to the side of the door. I go start the truck and wait for him. Once he's back in the truck, I look over to see him watching as Lilly walks down the sidewalk. He pulls out his phone and types something. She stops, pulls out her phone, looks at it, turns and looks over her shoulder, and gives him a smile that could make the sun jealous, before she turns back around and starts walking again.

"So, you got her number?"

"Yeah, she goes to school over here." He says pulling out a clean shirt from his bag.

"She seems shy," I say, pulling out onto the road.

"Liz is shy."

"No, Liz is observant."

"Whatever. So how are things with you and Liz?" I glance at my baby brother, debating what I should say. "You're still into her, right? If not, Johnny was asking about her." I look over, ready to let him know that I will fuck Johnny up if he even *thinks* about talking to Liz, when I see the smirk on his face. "Well, judging by the shade of red you just turned, I'm gonna say you're still with her."

"Yeah, and I'm staying with her; so tell anyone who asks to back the fuck off."

"Calm down! Damn! I thought that with her basically living with you, and you two buying a damn dog together, that it would calm your possessive ass down. Guess I was wrong." I look over to see him shaking his head. "Don't get me wrong, I love November and Liz, but I'm never going to let a female turn me into some kind of crazy, possessive, pussy-whipped guy." I almost laugh and warn him of what's going to happen when he meets the one, but fuck it; he can figure that shit out on his own, and I'll be laughing about it from the sidelines.

"Any word from Liz's brother?" he asks, changing the subject

"Nah, nothing. I called Kenton and asked him to look into it," I reply.

"Do you know why Nico's spending so much time with him?"

"He likes the bigger city." I shrug.

"I thought that too, but he mentioned the other day that he might go work for Kenton."

"Seriously?" Thinking of the work that my cousin does makes me nervous for my brother. My cousin's life is like something out of a movie. He's constantly on the road, looking for the people who everyone else runs away from. "When was he going to tell us?" I ask.

All of us boys own even shares in our construction business. Asher started the business up when he got out of the Marines, and each of us bought in after college. Since then, the business has grown, and now we have contracts all over Tennessee.

"He told me that Kenton had asked him to help out on a job the other day. He said he had never thought about doing that kind of thing, but when he was done, he couldn't stop thinking about it. I guess Kenton told him that he had a knack for it and would be willing to train him if he was interested in doing it for the long term," he says.

"So he's really considering it?"

"From what he said, yeah. I think he's just worried about what we'll all say."

"I don't like it; I know that what Kenton does is dangerous. But if he's happy, then how can I say no?"

"That's what I said." Cash's phone starts ringing. "Speak of the devil," he mutters. "Yo," he answers. "Are you serious?" Cash pauses, and I can tell he's concentrating on whatever is being said; then he starts laughing so hard that tears start streaming down his cheeks.

"What?" I ask.

"Shit man, hold on. Let me tell him." He shakes his head, trying to control himself. "Last night, Nico went to the restaurant over on 5th street. Well, when he pulled into the parking lot, it was after eleven, and Liz was standing next to her car covered in dirt, looking like she got caught with her hand in the cookie jar. Nico asked her what was going on, and she said she was just getting ready to go home." My heart drops, thinking that something happened to her.

"I talked to her before I went to bed. She was home and didn't tell me that anything happened to her."

"No, man, she's fine. She left the parking lot while Nico was there watching. Well, he went inside to

order out, and Jen was there with her friends."
Shit. This is what I didn't need fucking Jen.

"What did Jen do to her?" I demand.

Cash starts laughing again, and I'm about ready to stop the truck and kick his ass.

"Jen didn't do anything if what Nico thinks happened, happened. Your girl jacked Jen's tire from her car, and left that shit sitting on three wheels."

"What?" I whisper. I cannot picture my sweet Liz doing anything like that...ever.

"When Nico got his order, he went back out to his truck just as Jen and her posse were getting ready to leave. Jen started yelling from across the parking lot, so he went over to see what was going on. That's when he saw Jen's driver's side back tire missing, not even a jack or a brick holding that shit up. Then, Nico remembered the look on Liz's face and how dirty she looked when he pulled into the parking lot, and everything came together."

"You are joking, right?"

"Looks like sweet Liz has a little evil in her after all." Cash chuckles, making me laugh.

"Something must have happened. I can't see Liz doing that for no reason." I'm trying not to let my imagination run away from me. I would never hit a chick, but if Jen or any of her posse fucked with my girl, they would answer to me.

"Don't know, but wish I could be a fly on the wall when you ask her about it," Cash says, putting the phone back to his ear. A thought occurred to me, and I couldn't help but to ask.

"Did he tell Jen that he thought it was Liz?" I ask, holding the steering wheel tighter when Cash didn't say anything. I glance over at him.

"Do you think that any of us would tell any of those bitches shit? Fuck no! We wouldn't; you should know that."

"Look," I sigh, running my hands down my face, trying to find the right words. "If Jen has even a hint that it was Liz, she will go after her. I can't risk something happening to her; she has enough shit going on without adding to it."

"You love her."

"What?" I look over at him, and my eyes narrow.

"You fucking love her. Holy shit!"

I want to say, "fuck no; hell no", and that it's impossible to love someone after only a few weeks together; then I remind myself that we spent nine months together before July was born. We might not have been together every day, but most of my free time was filled with her. I didn't know it at the time, but I had been slowly falling in love with her. I'm snapped out of my thoughts by the speakerphone, with Nico singing, *"Da da da da, another one bites the dust. And another one falls, and another one falls, another one bites the dust."*

"Very funny," I sigh, rubbing the back of my head.

"Just saying. I don't want that shit to happen to me," Nico says, his voice coming through the cell phone in Cash's hand.

"You asses will be singing a different tune when it does."

"Fuck that. I'm going to get as much pussy as I can before I have to settle with one."

"I didn't even call to talk about this shit," Nico cuts Cash off. "I wanted to make sure that you were all going to be at the site tomorrow," Nico says, sounding nervous.

I look over at Cash, and can see the same pain I'm feeling written on his face. "Sure, we'll be there."

"Good, see you guys then," he says, before the line goes dead.

"So, I guess he's going to talk to us about working for Kenton."

"Guess so," I agree. I don't want to think about this shit right now. My brothers and I have always been inseparable, and I don't want to think about Nico not being a part of our company any more.

"So...you gonna call Liz and ask her about the tire?"

"Do I look stupid to you?"

"Yes," he chuckles, and I look over at him.

"I'll talk to her about it when I get home."

"You're sounding very domesticated these days."

"Fuck you," I say while smiling.

Cash shakes his head, laughing. "I'm going to stay away from chicks from now on. There must be something in the water."

"So you aint gonna call Lilly?"

"Fuck yeah, I'm calling her! Did you see her tits?" I look over at him; he's holding out his hands in front of him like he's got huge melons balancing in them.

"You're full of shit," I laugh. Out of all of us, Cash is the one who wears his heart on his sleeve.

"Never mind don't look at her tits." He says. I look over to see a look of confusion on his face before he ask "So are you and Liz living together?"

"Yes, but don't tell her I told you that."

"So you're living together but she doesn't know it?"

"Pretty much." I shrug.

He laughs. "Let me know how that works out for you."

~~*

It's after seven when I finally pull up to the house. Liz's car is in the driveway, so I decide to check her trunk. As soon as the trunk light comes on, I can see that she had pulled up the carpet to get to her spare, but there is no spare, and no extra tire that could have been Jen's. I look around, wondering where she would have put an extra tire.

"What are you doing?" I hear Liz ask from the front porch. I look up to see her arms crossed over her chest; Lolly is sitting calmly at her side.

"Hey, baby. Nico said you had a flat," I lie, and watch her face pale.

"Uh, yeah. I met November for dinner, and when I got out to my car, I had a flat." Her voice wavers a bit at the end, and I have to stop the smile from coming across my face.

"Where is your spare?" I ask, slamming the trunk. I walk around to my truck and pull my bag from the back. Lolly finally decides to come off the porch, but Liz Is stuck in place.

"The spare?" She looks around like it's going to appear out of thin air. Cute. I shake my head, then bend down to pet Lolly.

"It's sad that you come to me before my girl does," I tell Lolly. Standing, I walk slowly towards Liz. "Yeah, baby. The spare tire for your car."

"Oh, that! Um...I had to leave it at the tire place." I can tell she's lying when she doesn't make eye contact.

"Well, I need to get a new tire for my truck tomorrow, so I'll just pick yours up when I go."

"That's really not necessary," she mumbles, barely loud enough for me to hear.

"It's no problem." I lean forward and grab her wrist, pulling her to me. "You haven't kissed me," I say, putting my face in her neck and breathing her in. I missed her smell; and as I lift my head, our eyes meet.

"You know, don't you?" she whispers, tears filling her beautiful eyes.

"Let's say Nico put two and two together." I watch her lip start to tremble. "Hey, what's that about?" Using my thumb, I swipe the tears from her cheeks.

"It's not my fault!" she cries, her face landing in my chest. I drop my bag, pick her up, and take her inside. I walk to the couch and sit with her in my lap.

"Talk to me." I say quietly, rubbing her back. Her breaths are heavy before answering. Then she tells me the whole story about Jen and her friends laughing, saying her name, and leaving the restaurant, and then how she found her tire slashed.

"You know that my car is always unlocked?" I nod; I do know that she never locks her car. I hate that shit. "Well, when I popped my trunk to get the spare tire, there wasn't one in there. Then I looked at my phone to call someone, and I had no service. So I looked around and noticed Jen's car, and for the first time I realized that we had the exact same car." She sits up and looks at me. "I was so mad. She has always been evil, but ever since we got together, it has gotten a million times worse. So I took my jack out of the trunk, went to her car, got her tire off, realized that I would need the jack to change my tire, so I kicked the jack out from under her car, ran back to my car, changed the tire as fast as I could—which by the way is pretty damn fast." I smile because she says all of this in one breath; she's so fucking adorable. Her eyes drop to my mouth, and her finger comes up to trace my lips. "I love your smile," she whispers, and I kiss her finger, making her smile. "Well, once I got the tire changed, and the slashed one put in my trunk, Nico pulled up and asked if I was okay. I started feeling guilty about what I had done, so this morning when I got up, I went and had my tire fixed and put back on my car. Then I took Jen's tire back to her house, made sure no one was around, and left it next to her garage.

"Jesus." I shake my head, close my eyes, and lean my head back on the couch.

"I feel bad enough already," she grumbles, making me laugh.

"This isn't funny!" she cries.

I open my eyes and end up laughing harder. "You're wrong; this is hilarious! I can't believe my sweet Liz could do something so evil." I raise an eyebrow. She shoves her face into her hands.

"I'm a horrible person," she mumbles.

"Hell no! You were doing what you had to do, and that bitch deserved it."

"I could have gone back into the restaurant and called someone," she says with a pout.

I lean forward, taking her face in my hands. "She shouldn't have slashed your tire."

"What if it wasn't even her who did it?" she asks, and I shake my head. Jen is manipulative; I don't put anything past her.

"Well, consider it Karma for her being such a bitch."

"Stop calling her that; you used to be with her."

"Baby," I say softly, pulling her closer. "We slept together; we were never in a relationship."

"I know that, but you still slept with her." I can hear the anger in her voice, and I'm not sure if she's mad that I called Jen a bitch, or if she's upset that I slept with her. All I know is that I'm going to tread lightly and change the subject.

"Did you miss me?" I start to pull her forward, but she resists, pulling away and getting off my lap.

"The way you treat women is so disgusting."

"What?" I choke out.

"I know that you hear what I'm saying, Trevor," she glares. "You treat women like crap."

"Have I ever treated you lik—?"

"Yes!" She cuts me off, walking close, and putting her finger in my face. "You ignored me when I tried to explain what I had meant when I said the word 'never' to you. Then you were an ass and didn't talk to me. Oh wait, that's not true." Her head goes back, and her fists clench. I wonder if it's wrong that I'm totally turned the fuck on right now. "You did talk to me, right? If a guy tried to talk to me, you growled at me...and him."

"Where is this all coming from?"

"What happens when you're done with me? What happens then? Will you tell people that I'm a bitch like you called Jen?"

"Fuck me!" I whisper-hiss.

"Exactly!"

That's it. I'm done. I grab her around the waist, pulling her to me. Then I pick her up, and carry her to the bedroom. Lolly barks once before she sits when I shoot her a death glare. I walk to the bedroom with a struggling and hissing Liz, toss her on the bed, and hold her ankle so she can't get away.

"Let me go." She twists, trying to crawl across the bed, so I climb up on the bed behind her covering her with my body, pressing her into the mattress. She's breathing heavy, her eyes closed tight with frustration.

"Now that you said what you needed to say, it's my turn to talk."

"I don't have a choice, do I? I can't get up; you're a bully," she says on a huff.

I bite my tongue to keep from laughing. "You ready to listen?" I whisper near her ear, feeling her shiver and go completely still. I'm sure she can feel my dick pressed into her back.

"Whatever," she mutters, making me smile.

"This is the last time we're going to bring up what happened that night." I press into her and she nods. "I never told you that when I stopped that night, I did it because I was afraid of my own feelings for you. I figured if I told myself that you were innocent, I would stop craving you." I press myself deeper into her back. "That didn't work. Every time a guy tried to talk to you, I wanted to beat the fuck out of him, or drag you off." I take a breath and lace my fingers through hers. "Now, as for Jen, I can tell you from experience that she is a *bitch*." I watch Liz flinch, so I roll her over and hold her face in my hands. "I don't say that about all the women I've been with, but I know Jen. I know that she uses her dad's influence to get away with a lot of shit." I press my forehead to hers. "As for you, I could never say that about you; even if I was

160

pissed, I know the kind of person you are. I know that you care about people, even the ones you shouldn't." She leans up, pressing her mouth to mine. "We done fighting now?" I ask, my hands running down along her sides.

"Yes," she whispers, then bites her lip.

Chapter 6

<u>Liz</u>

I don't know why I was so mad at him for saying that about Jen, but I hate that word. I think what I'm really mad about is my brother's phone call. This time, he didn't call me; he called my mom to tell her that he wasn't coming home before flying to Jamaica, but that he would meet us there. My mom now thinks that he is working undercover with the police. How he convinced her that he was doing that kind of work, I have no clue; but the look of pride of my mother's face when she came into the shop to tell me that she had spoken with Tim had been gut wrenching.

"What's going on in that head of yours?" I look up into Trevor's eyes and notice that he's watching me closely.

"My brother called my mom."

"That's good, right?" I shake my head, biting my lip. Whatever is going on with Tim, I know now that it's not good. It's bad, really, really bad.

"He told my mom that he started working undercover for the police."

"He what?" Trevor growls, "You need to tell your mom what's going on. I understand why you didn't want to before, but this is getting out of hand."

"The wedding is this weekend. I can't tell her now. When we get back, I'll talk to her." He shakes his head. "I don't want her to be stressed about this right before her wedding."

"If your brother shows up in Jamaica, I'm going to beat the shit out of him. Not only has he stolen money from you, now he's playing your mom."

"I know," I whisper, not wanting to deal with this, but knowing that I have to. "When Mom gets back from her honeymoon, I will sit her down and talk to her about what's going on."

"I don't like it."

"Well, too bad; it's not your choice. It has nothing to do with you."

"Nothing to do with me?" His eyes narrow and I look away. "You are mine; that means that it has everything to do with me."

I shrug. I know that it's pointless to argue with him. In Trevor's universe, he is right, I'm wrong, and there will be no convincing him any different. "Look at me, Liz." His voice is quiet, so my eyes automatically go to his. "If something happens to you because of your brother, I will kill him. No joke. I will rip him apart with my bare hands." I can feel my eyes widen; that is not what I expected him to say. "Like I said before, I don't like this shit. And if something happens to you because you refuse to tell your mom, I'm going to spank your ass."

My eyes narrow. "If you ever even think about spanking me, I'm going to beat the crap out of you, Trevor."

His eyebrow rises. "You think you can take me?"

"No." I shrug. "But I will give it my best shot."

His smile is so devastating that it takes my breath. "When you're giving it your best shot, are our clothes on or off?"

I roll my eyes. "Get off me, you perv." I start to struggle to get up, but then I feel Trevor's mouth open on my neck, and his hand travel down my side. His thumb brushes against my breast, then down to the hem of my shirt, and back up under. I feel the roughness of his palm against the softness of my waist. *Oh my God, yes!* My brain screams. I love him touching me. He sits back, pulling my shirt up and over my head; his eyes go to my black full-lace bra, then come back to mine.

"I missed you," he says softly, and then he kisses me. My mouth automatically opens under his; he tastes like heaven, and I want to consume him. He pulls his mouth away from mine, licking and biting down my neck to my breast. His fingers trace the edge of my bra; he tugs the cup down, licks, then blows on my nipple, making me moan and arch into him. My body starts shaking as soon as his mouth latches onto my nipple and he sucks hard, making me rise off the bed; my hands go to his head, holding on tight. As his hand travels down my waist, I can feel him unbutton my jeans. Then his fingers are sliding through my wetness, one entering me as I moan loudly, circling my hips.

"Yes," I whisper, as he hits my g-spot. He stops and pulls his mouth away; my eyes open. He's looking down at me. I want to cry. He keeps doing this, always stopping when I want to go.

"I'm hungry," he says, pulling his hand out of my pants. I start to sit up, confused and wondering if I was the only one involved in what just happened.

"You're hungry?" I repeat what he just said, thinking this was strange. I thought we were going to have sex. I might not have a ton of experience, but I know the signs, and they are all flashing neon red with arrows pointing at my vajayjay... and he's hungry?

"Very hungry," he says, standing up. I start to look around for my shirt, because apparently, we were going to go get something to eat! Well, he is going to get something to eat; I'm going to find a way to kill him without going to jail. My head is turned when I feel his hand at the waistband of my jeans. He yanks and pulls them off. I'm startled and then pulled not-too-gently to the edge of the bed. There's no time to prepare before he attacks me, his mouth latching onto my clit. The heels of my feet go to his shoulders; my hips lift, and my fingers grab onto the top of his head.

"Yes," I moan, lifting and grinding my hips.

"You taste so good, baby." His hands go under my ass, lifting me closer to his mouth. I start breathing heavy, feeling like I'm getting ready to fall off a cliff. "Come for me," he whispers as he licks me, circling my clit. I'm so close; I just need something else.

"More," I whimper, not able to form a complete sentence.

"What do you want?" he asks against me, his voice rough. I can feel the stubble of his jaw scraping against my skin.

"You. I need you!" I cry. He drops my ass, spreads my legs further apart, then two fingers enter me, pulling up against my g-spot so quickly that I shoot off the bed with the force of the orgasm that explodes through me. I fly apart while seeing stars; my body's on fire, every nerve feeling exposed. When I finally come back to myself, Trevor's above me, his clothes gone.

"You're so beautiful," he whispers, taking my mouth in a deep kiss. He pulls me forward, removing my bra. I can feel his body press against mine, his hard muscles covered by smooth skin, his weight pressing me into the mattress, his size surrounding me, making me feel fragile and safe. He pulls his mouth away from mine and he looks at me. I can see the same desire coursing through me in his eyes. "My turn," he says against my lips. Before I can ask what he means, he's slamming into me. My legs circle his hips; my nails dig into his biceps. My head flies back, my body arching. "Jesus," he grunts, stilling his movements, his forehead laying against my chest. "So perfect." He slides out, then back in slower.

"Finally," I breathe. I have wanted this for so long, and finally having it is like every holiday rolled into one. He starts to speed up, his hand traveling down my side, all the way to my knee and he pulls it up; I can feel him deeper. He's so thick and long that every time he fills me, I bite my lip against the slight sting. I can feel myself tighten around him; I'm getting close.

"I fucking knew I'd love your pussy, baby," he says, sitting up on his calves, pulling me up with him so we're face-to-face. "Wrap your legs around me." I do what he says. His hands slide up my thighs, to my ass, waist, and ribs; one stays there while the other tangles into my hair. "Move with me." He pulls down on my chin with his mouth so I'll let go of my lip. We start rocking together very slowly, his eyes never leaving mine. "Are you mine, Liz?" he whispers his question, and I nod my head. "I need to hear you tell me that your mine." I swallow; for some reason this feels like something else, more serious than the 'will you be my girlfriend' question. "Say it, Liz. Tell me that you're mine."

"I'm yours," I whisper, feeling like I just gave a giant piece of me away to him, knowing that it's something I can't take back.

"That's right, baby. You're mine; don't ever forget it," he says harshly, before he starts lifting his hips harder and faster. I bite down on his shoulder to keep myself from screaming out. When I feel myself tighten around him, he pulls my face out of his neck, and slams his mouth against mine. His other hand goes to my breast, pinching my nipple, sending me over. I hear him rumble my name, following behind me with his own orgasm. We're both breathing heavy, my face tucked under his chin, his arms wrapped around me. I can't help the laugh that bubbles out. "Why are you laughing?" I can hear the smile in his voice.

"Just thinking that you proved a whole lot of people wrong."

"What?" He asks, bending back so that I'm now sprawled on top of him. He pulls my hair away from my face, tracing my eyebrows. I look in his eyes; they are so warm that I can hardly breathe. "What?" he asks, more quietly this time.

I shake my head, clearing my mind. "You know the old saying? Guys who drive big trucks have—" He rolls us over so I'm under him, and he grits his teeth, sliding out of me.

"Don't finish that thought." He shakes his head, chuckling.

"What? You don't have that problem." I laugh when he starts tickling me. "Okay! Okay! I won't talk about it!" I yell.

He stops his torture, his elbow going into the bed next to my head. "You ready to get out of town?"

"Yes. Plus, I'm excited. My mom is the happiest I have ever seen her."

"George is a good guy," he nods.

"Yeah, he is," I agree. My mom met George two years ago online. George had been divorced for four years; he waited until his youngest was in college before he started looking for a relationship. He had gone on a few blind dates and nothing ever worked out. One day, he was home watching TV and a commercial about an online dating site came on. He said "what the hell", and signed up. That was around the time I signed my mom up behind her back. I wanted her to be happy. I hated seeing her so lonely; she deserved to find someone. Shortly after I signed her up, George sent her a message. That's when I told her about the site and what I did. At first, she didn't want to write him back, but I convinced her that if she didn't like what he said through e-mail, that she never had to speak with him again. So she took a chance, and after a few e-mails and phone calls, they met up. He lives about an hour from us in Alabama, and since their first meeting, they have been inseparable.

"I'm going to talk to George about what's going on."

"No, you're not!"

"He needs to know in case something happens."

I narrow my eyes, "What could my brother possibly do?"

"Did you ask yourself what he could possibly do before he stole your money? Then called you needing more? He's calling your mom, saying he's working undercover; do you not see how fucking serious this is?"

"Yes, I fucking see how serious this is!" I yell, stand up on the bed, and look down on Trevor where he's lying. "He is my brother; the same one who took care of me after my dad died." I can feel my chest heaving up and down. "So excuse me if I don't want to call the police or tell my mom. I'm trying to help him the only way he asked; he said he needed more time, so that's what I'm giving him." I jump off the bed. Realizing that I'm Naked, I stomp to the dresser and grab a shirt. Stomping into the bathroom, I slam the door and turn on the shower.

"Don't walk away when we're talking." I hear him say as he opens the door.

"*You* were talking, Mr. Know-It-All," I say, pulling the shower curtain closed behind me. I grab my shampoo, squeezing half the bottle into my hand out of anger, that pisses me off even more; its expensive shampoo, and you're only supposed to use a little. I hear the curtain slide back, but I ignore it, and continue washing my hair.

"You're pissing me off, baby."

"You're pissing me off, baby," I mimic. I can't help it; he makes me so mad that I revert back to being five-years-old. I hear him laugh, and I want to punch him.

"Have I ever told you how cute you are when you're pissed?" I open one eye to look at him.

Sure enough, he has a big smile on his face. He takes a step towards me, his hands going to my hair. "I know you love your brother, baby, but you need to know that if something happens because you keep trying to protect everyone, you're going to end up feeling like shit, because you could have said something."

I know he's right, but I'm torn. My brother and I were close after my dad died and my mom closed down. He was all I had for so long. I close my eyes, my forehead going into Trevor's chest. He steps us back so I'm under the showerhead and starts rinsing my hair. He then leans over me, grabs my conditioner, squeezes the bottle, and then his hands are massaging it into my hair. "I know you're right," I whisper, guilt eating me alive. "I keep praying that Tim will come home and do the right thing, but deep down, I don't think that's going to happen. But I don't want to give up on him either."

"You're not giving up on your brother. You're giving him a chance, and letting the people who could end up hurt prepare."

"How can I want to kiss you and punch you at the same time?" I ask, shaking my head.

"You're kinky like that," he says, tilting my head back. Before I can say something smart, his mouth touches mine, his hands travel down my sides to my ass, and he lifts me, my legs circling his hips. "I didn't use a condom earlier," he says against my lips. I freeze, pulling my mouth away from his. "I'm clean." He turns, pressing me against the tile.

I swallow; why didn't I think about that? I shake my head. "I'm on birth control," I say, more as a reminder to myself. Then he thrust inside me. "November got pregnant when she was on birth control," I say out loud to myself again, then moan when he withdraws, only to press inside me harder than before. My head falls back against the tile. He doesn't say anything, just continues to slam inside of me, his mouth sucking and licking my neck, collarbone, and breast. When his teeth scrape against my nipple, I feel myself start to come around him; my nails dig into his shoulders, my legs tightening, pulling him deeper.

"Jesus, you have the tightest, smoothest fucking pussy." His hands squeeze my ass harder, lifting and pulling me down on him in fast rapid thrusts. "This is what heaven must feel like," he grunts, his pace becoming more erratic. I can feel him hitting against my cervix, the slight pain bringing me closer to another orgasm. When I feel him start to expand, I come again, leaning forward, biting down hard on his shoulder. We're both breathing heavy when my mouth lifts away from his skin.

"I'm sorry." I touch where my teeth marks are imprinted into his skin.

"Don't be. I love that I can make you lose control. That's how I want you. That's how you make me feel; it's only fair that I make you feel the same."

"You're always in control."

"Not with you." His jaw clenches, his eyes looking angry.

"Is it so bad?" I ask, looking over his face.

"Not always," he looks at the tile wall behind me. "Unless you consider locking someone away so that no one can touch them a 'bad thing'."

"I think they call that kidnapping." I smile and he shakes his head, his eyes coming to mine.

"You are the one thing that scares me. Your power over me scares me."

"You scare me, too." I lay my head against his shoulder. He lifts me up and I feel him slide out; he kisses my hair, then let's go of my legs so I slide down his body, and when my feet hit the floor of the shower, I take a minute to get stable. Trevor's hands hold my face as he kisses my forehead, nose, and lips.

"You will always be safe with me." I am not sure if he is right; I know that there will come a time when he will want more than what I can offer him. It wouldn't be fair of me to keep him from having a family, even if it killed me that I couldn't be the one giving it to him. "Are you off tomorrow?"

I shake my head. I can't talk over the lump in my throat. As he takes his time washing me, he's very gentle between my legs. Once he's done, I step out of the shower, making sure not to look at him as I grab a towel. I put it to my face, taking a few deep breaths. "Do you work tomorrow?" I ask, as I lift my head once I know I've gotten myself under control.

"Yeah, I should be home early. When do you get off?"

"Well, Mom left today, and tomorrow is my last day until the day after we get home. Bambi's going to be looking over the store while we're gone, and November is going to help out as well."

"Are you sure you should trust Bambi?" he asks, as we walk out of the bathroom into the bedroom.

I laugh and his eyes narrow. "Oh stop. Just because she is immune to the Mayson men's charms, doesn't mean she is a bad person."

"You trust people too easily."

"November is going to be there with her for part of the day. I need to have people I can trust with my business, or I'm going to end up never having a break."

"I'm going to see if my mom can go over a couple of the days."

"Trevor—uh—what's your middle name? How do I not know this?" I bite my lip and try to remember if I have ever heard it anywhere before.

"Sorry, that's top secret information," he smirks, walking to the dresser; my eyes follow him as the muscles of his thighs and back stretch and expand, showing off the tribal tattoo that travels up his wrist, under his collar bone, down his chest, over his ribs, along his side, down his hip, and ending on his thigh. I love that tattoo. I want to lick it and trace it with my tongue; each step he takes makes my mouth water. When he looks over his shoulder at me, I look away, quickly pulling my towel tighter around my body. Until that second, I've never felt self-conscious about the way I look. Looking at him now, with not one ounce of fat on him, I'm thinking I should start to do some sit-ups, or maybe a few squats. "You keep thinking all those dirty thoughts, baby, and I'm going to be ripping your towel off and fucking you against the wall."

"I wasn't having dirty thoughts. Not all of them were dirty anyways." I mumble under my breath. I walk to my bag that is shoved under the bed, pull it out, grab a pair of panties, and slide them up under my towel. Then I find a tank top and slip that on over my head, removing the towel from under it. I bend to find a pair of shorts. I start to lift my foot to put them on, when they're snatched out of my hand. "Hey! I'm going to wear those!" I yell, glaring at Trevor, who has my shorts balled in his fist.

"As sexy as that show was," he says, shaking his head, "you're in my house. I've finger fucked you, eaten your pussy, and been inside you without a rubber. You are not going to hide your body from me."

"You're such a jerk," I say, feeling my face burning bright red.

"Only because you're not getting your way," he shrugs, tossing my shorts on the bed, before walking out of the room. I'm reaching across the bed to grab my shorts when my ass is slapped, then I'm tossed over his bare shoulder and carried to the kitchen, where he puts me on the counter. My brain is still trying to catch up with what just happened; I can't even form a full thought. "You want a sandwich?" he asks causally, walking over to the fridge. He starts to pull out lunchmeat and cheese; he sets them next to me before going to grab the bread. "Do you want a sandwich?" he asks again.

I look at him, getting ready to scream my head off and tell him that he is not the boss of me, he can't tell me what to do, what to wear, or carry me around whenever he feels like it. Just as I'm about to flip the hell out, I hear the dog door open. I look over, expecting to see Lolly, but instead, I see a little pink nose poke inside, then a small, round, black head. I blink a few times, trying to see if I have somehow imagined this, then a long, black body, with a white stripe down the center, starts to climb the rest of the way inside.

"Trevor," I whisper, trying to get his attention. His head is in the fridge so he doesn't hear me. "Trevor," I whisper a little louder this time, as I start to get up on the counter. The skunk is now near Lolly's dog dish, where he starts to eat the food. "Oh my God!" I cry, covering my mouth.

Trevor turns around; he looks up at me and smiles. "You gonna attack me?"

I frantically start shaking my head no. He walks over to me, and growls, "Jesus, this is the perfect position for me to eat the fuck out of your sweet pussy." He slides his hands up the back of my calves. His face going between my legs, I can feel him take a deep breath.

"Trevor," I whisper again, trying to push his face away with one hand.

"What?" He tilts his head back; his eyebrows come together when he looks up at me. My mouth is still covered. I point over his shoulder, and he turns his head and looks down.

"What the fuck?" he says, jumping, stumbling back, banging into the counter, and then his hands go to the counter behind him. He jumps so that he's standing on top of it with me. "That's a skunk," he says, taking a step back from the edge of the counter.

"No shit, Sherlock!" I laugh, still covering my mouth. I can't help it; the look on his face is hilarious. His eyes narrow and I bite my lip to keep from cracking up. I do not want to set the skunk off. "You need to get rid of it," I tell him, looking down at the skunk, who is happily chowing away on the dog food.

"What am I supposed to do?"

"I have no idea. You're the one who has the penis, and the one who likes to boss everyone around all the time; I'm sure you can figure it out."

"You still pissed about not wearing your shorts?"

"Oh my God, Trevor!" I hiss, "There is a skunk." I fling my arm out to show him the skunk, in case he forgot. "You want to talk about this right now?"

"Baby," he laughs, "Calm down." He pulls my face towards him by the back of my neck and kisses me. When he pulls his mouth from mine, we're both breathing heavily. "I love your lips," he says, biting my lower lip, giving it a tug.

"The skunk." I remind the two of us. Leaning into him, he pulls away, looking down at the ground. The skunk is looking up at us, where we're standing on the counter. "Where is Lolly?" I ask. The skunk hasn't moved from its spot on the floor where he's staring at us.

"I don't know. Hopefully she doesn't come inside right now."

"What are we going to do?" I whisper. The skunk starts walking around the kitchen, then slowly makes it way to the dog door, where he pauses, looks up at us again, and starts to lift its tail. I bury my face in Trevor's chest.

"It's gone," Trevor says, after a second, he jumps off the counter, walking towards the dog door. Just then, the dog door starts to push open, and Trevor flies back towards me, hopping on the counter as Lolly shoves through the door. "Holy shit," he sighs in relief, jumping down from the counter again, running to the door, and sliding the latch in place. "Looks like we're going to have to start making sure to lock this when it's dark."

"I can't believe that just happened." I hop off the counter and go over to Lolly, who is scratching at the dog door, trying to find a way to break out.

"I wonder if that's the first time we had an uninvited guest," Trevor says, going to the sink to wash his hands.

"I don't even want to know; can you imagine getting up in the middle of the night to get a glass of water, and getting sprayed by a skunk in the process."

"Hell no. Guess that's the price you pay for living in the country."

"Why did you buy this place?" I love this house, but it needs work.

"The land; I wanted something outside of town, where I could have a party or ride my dirt bike without having to worry about neighbors." He walks across the kitchen, grabbing my hips, lifting me back onto the counter.

"You really need to stop toting me around," I glare at him.

"Why?" He looks at me like I just asked him to stop showering for a month. I take a deep breath.

"I don't like it."

"Yes, you do." He walks across the kitchen, getting the bread out of the breadbox.

"Actually, I hate it when you do it." I don't really hate it, but I do find it annoying a lot of times when I'm trying to do something, and he just carries me off or moves me without giving me a chance to do what I want.

"You don't hate it." "You want to know how I know you don't hate it?" He looks at me, raising an eyebrow.

"This should be good," I mumble, watching him make his sandwich. I'm half tempted to stop him from finishing. He doesn't even make sure that the mayo and mustard are spread evenly on the bread; he just globs it on there. I look up when he starts laughing. "What?"

"Like this. This is killing you; I see it in your face that you want to hop off the counter, take this out of my hands, and do it yourself."

"So?" I cross my arms over my chest.

"You don't get your way, and you want to throw a fit."

"That's not true."

"Yeah, babe. It is."

"Whatever," I say, as he comes to stand between my legs, pulling me closer to the edge of the counter.

"You need to learn that not everything has to be done when or how you want it done. It's okay to give up some of the control that you try to hold onto so tightly. With me, I'm not asking, I'm telling you how it is. It doesn't mean that I don't respect you or care about the way you feel; it just means that you trust me enough to make sure that you've got what you need."

"I'm feeling a little lost. I thought we were talking about you manhandling me."

"We were, and we are. I told you that you don't hate it when I tell you what to do, or put you where I want you. And the reason I know you don't hate it is because you listen or stay where I put you every time." Holy shit. He's right. What the hell is wrong with me? "Now, do you want me to make you a sandwich?"

"No thanks." I don't want to encourage his dominant behavior. I want to go somewhere and have a tantrum.

"Okay." He kisses my forehead, and goes back to what he's doing with me watching. The rest of the night, I think about what he said, and my need for control. I don't know if he knows it, but with him, I have none. When we get into bed, he pulls me under him like he always does, kisses my temple, and goes to sleep. I realize that we didn't talk anymore after our conversation in the kitchen. Like he wanted me to think about everything that he said. I huff out a breath, determined to stop thinking about everything; he can't be the boss of my subconscious. Then I fall asleep, thinking that I'm comfortable, warm, and safe, so maybe giving him control isn't so bad.

Chapter 7

Trevor

I look out the double doors of our room at the resort and can see the turquoise sea beyond. There's a slight breeze coming in off of the water, bringing the sound and smell of the ocean with it. I roll to my side; Liz is laying on her stomach, hands under her pillow, a sheet resting over her hips. My hand itches to touch her. I scrub my hands down my face, thinking about yesterday, and wondering if today is going to be better or worse.

When we arrived last night, Liz's mom, Rita, was waiting for us in the lobby. She looked worried. I assumed she was nervous about the wedding. Then Tim walked around the corner into the lobby. When I saw him, I felt the urge to beat the shit out of him; if I hadn't promised Liz I would be on my best behavior when I was around Tim, I would have had him face first on the very expensive tile. Instead, I bit down on the inside of my cheek, trying to check the impulse of attack. Tim walked over to our group. He avoided eye contact with me; his eyes focused on his sister. When he reached her, he picked her up and hugged her. I could hear him say something to her, but couldn't make out the words until she told him to be nice. Tim turned towards me after he sat Liz down; that's when I noticed the girl with him. She was small, with short black hair and big brown eyes. She looked like a pixie. The part that caught my attention was her stomach; she had to be around five months pregnant. Tim put his arm around her, pulling her close.

"Trevor." He stuck out his hand, and I did the same. Our shake was not friendly. We were both stating that we could take the other one out. Tim was not a small guy; he played football in high school and still looked to be in shape. He pulled his hand away first, making me feel like I won that challenge.

"Liz, Trevor, I want you to meet Kara," Tim said, looking over at Liz, who was looking down at the girls protruding belly.

"Kara," Liz said. I took a step closer to her; she looked ready to pass out.

"I told Tim that I shouldn't come, but he said he couldn't stand the thought of me being home by myself," Kara said, smiling at Liz. The Liz that I used to know, the one on guard from everyone around her, slipped into place. She took Kara's hand in her own, shaking it lightly. That's when Liz noticed the ring on Kara's hand.

"My mom's wedding ring," Liz said, looking at the ring on her finger, running her thumb over the gold band.

"Tim asked me to marry him when he got home from his last visit. Right, babe?" she asked, looking up at him. I could tell by the way she looked at him that she really loved him.

"Congratulations," Liz said, looking up at Tim.

"Thanks. I wanted to tell you guys a long time ago, but with the wedding, I didn't know how to bring it up." Tim had enough remorse to look guilty when Liz looked at him. Why did he claim to have an addiction, steal her money, and not tell his family about his fiancée? I looked at Liz's mom and noticed that she was nervous.

I could see Liz take a deep breath, and I know I need to get her out of this situation as soon as possible.

"It's nice to meet you, Kara," I said, pulling Liz deeper into my side. Liz's arm came around my back, her nails digging into my ribs.

"You too. We will see you guys in the morning for breakfast." I couldn't get her away from her brother fast enough. We said our goodbyes to Rita, Kara, and Tim. I picked up our bags and stepped in front of a dazed Liz. "Come on babe," I said quietly, then headed towards the elevators.

"We'll see you in the morning, honey," Rita said, giving Liz a quick hug. I looked back over my shoulder, and slowed down when I noticed she was still a ways behind me. When we made eye contact, I could see so much pain flash through her eyes that I had to stop myself from picking her up and taking her away from all of it.

"You hungry?" I asked, dropping one of the bags onto the floor of the elevator so I could touch her.

"No," she said, cuddling her face into my hand.

I pulled her forward by her jaw and kissed her softly. What I wanted to do was tell her that I loved her, but once again, I didn't. I couldn't. "You wanna take a walk down by the ocean with me?"

"I just want to go to sleep," she said. I pulled her into my chest, kissing the top of her head. When the elevator came to a stop, I let her off ahead of me, picked up our bags, and headed down the hall to our room. When she came to a stop, opened the door, and just stood there, I thought something was wrong, until she looked over at me smiling. I followed her into the room. The bathroom was right inside the door, with a Jacuzzi tub, stand up shower, and double sinks. The rest of the room was open, with a king sized bed with tall posters and a white canopy. There were side tables, a dresser with a flat screen TV on it, and a chair next to the open doors that led to a balcony. Outside, there was a large couch and a small table. The minute I saw that balcony, I knew I was going to find a way to fuck Liz out there while looking out over the ocean. "This is so beautiful." I dropped the bags to the ground, walking out to the balcony behind her.

"It is," I agreed, pulling her back to my front. Leaning over her, my face went into her neck, smelling the scent of her hair mixed with the ocean. "You wanna talk about what happened down in the lobby?"

She was quiet for a long time, just looking out over the ocean. I didn't think she was going to say anything, until she spoke. "He gave her my mom's wedding ring; the one my dad gave my mom."

"I know."

"Why did he steal the money and make up all of those lies?"

"I don't know, but tomorrow you can ask him."

"Can't you just go cut off his head and bring it back to me?"

"Real funny," I pulled her deeper into me. "I'm thinking that about ten seconds after I showed up here with his head, you would start feeling guilty." I kiss the top of her head, and look back out over the water.

"You're right. Damn conscience." She took a deep breath. "Thank you for being here with me." Her words were so quiet that I almost missed them, and once again, the words "I love you" were on the tip of my tongue.

"There is nowhere else I would want to be."

"I think I'm going to call room service and order something big and chocolaty."

"Alright. I'm going to go talk to George." Before she could start her protest, I reminded her, "You promised, so don't even think about starting a fight."

"I never promised."

"Did you tell me that you were mine?"

"Trevor, you know that I never agreed for you to talk to George."

"You told me you were mine. So yes, you did agree for me to talk to George."

"You are so annoying." She stepped around me, and back into the room.

I stopped her, pulled her into me, grabbed the back of her head, and twisted my hand into her hair, holding her in place so my mouth was right above hers. "When I get back, I'll give you the orgasm you're itchin' for," I told her, my mouth opening over hers. She fought it for a second, before melting into the kiss.

She tasted like strawberries from the Tic Tac's she'd been eating. I loved that taste; it made me kiss her harder and deeper. I had to pull myself away before I pulled her dress up and I fucked her up against the wall. Her eyes slowly opened. "Be back." I kissed her forehead. I needed to get away before I attacked her again. I looked over my shoulder; when I got to the door, she was still in the same place I left her, making me smile. She shrugged as I pulled the door closed behind me.

When I got to George and Rita's room, Rita answered, telling me that George was down in the cigar bar with his brother, so I headed down there. Once I found him, I filled him in on Tim, and the things he had told Liz. While we were talking, he told me about Tim, and his arrival yesterday with Kara.

He told me that Rita knew he was going to ask Kara to marry him, but didn't want to tell Liz until they met in person. George was pissed about the money, and said he was going to talk to Tim about it after the wedding. He didn't want to upset Rita or Liz any more than necessary. I agreed with him, and headed back up to the room, where I found Liz sitting outside on the balcony, eating what was left of some chocolate cake.

"Hey." I walked over to her, getting a chocolate kiss.

"So do you feel better now that you talked to George?" she asked as I'm sitting down.

"Yep."

"You smell like smoke."

"George was in the cigar bar downstairs. How about that bath?" I asked, picking her up and carrying her into the bathroom.

"You're awake?" Liz says, snapping me out of my thoughts. I lift my eyes to her still-sleepy face. Her hair's a mess, and her skin is clean of makeup; this is my favorite look on her. After we got out of the bath last night, I laid her out in bed, and spent a good amount of time appreciating her.

"Yeah, I've been up for a while now." I run my hands down my face.

"Couldn't sleep?" She comes up on her elbows, the sheet sliding lower down her hips, her long hair covering one breast, leaving the other exposed.

"What?" I swallow. I feel like a prick; all I can think about when I'm around her is fucking her. It doesn't help that she has nothing on but the sheet.

"You couldn't sleep?" she asks again, this time with a smirk, lifting her ass slightly off the bed.

"You're really asking for it, aren't you?"

"I have no idea what you're talking about, Mr. Mayson." She smiles, licking her lips, while looking down my chest to the sheet that is now tented.

"I'm trying to behave," I tell her, and my hand clenches.

"Hmm, you do that then," she says, pulling the sheet up over her head. I see her scoot towards me, then feel her mouth wrap around my cock. I almost come right then.

"Shit." My hands go above my head. I don't want her to stop, so I don't touch her. I can tell that she's kneeling under the sheet, and I feel her moan against me. I pull the sheet away to see her mouth and hand wrapped around me, her other hand between her legs. "Jesus." I pull her ass towards me so I can watch as she plays with herself. "Is it turning you on to suck me off, baby?" She moans, her fingers moving a little faster. I twist her more so that I have the perfect shot of her wet pussy. "You gonna let me clean you up with my mouth after you make yourself come?" I can feel her whimper as she takes me all the way, until I hit the back of her throat. My spine starts to tingle. "I'm going to come," I say, giving her a chance to retreat before one hand goes to her hair, and the other to her pussy. I come in her mouth as I put two fingers inside her. I can feel her start to come around them. I lift her up so she's sitting on my face, her hands going to the wall behind my head. I wait until she looks down at me before I do one long sweep of my tongue.

"Oh my God," she says, her head falling back.

"Play with your tits while I eat you." She does as I say, her hands going to her breasts, and then pulling her nipples. Without realizing it, she starts grinding down on my face. I grab her ass in my hands, pulling her tighter against me. When I know she's about to come, I lift her, and then impale her on my cock. She yells, and her muscles contract around me. "You're so fucking hot," I groan, pulling her down as I lift up to pound into her. "Give me your mouth." I tell her. She does, leaning forward, and I feel her start to convulse. And just like that, I'm shouting her name, coming inside of her as her pussy milks me. She lays against my chest; we're both breathing heavy, with me still inside of her. I love this. I love being inside of her, feeling her wrapped around me in every way. I run my hands down her back, pulling her hair to one side. "Are you okay?"

"Umhmm." I smile when I feel her cheek move against my chest.

"What do you want to do today?"

"Mom and I have an appointment at the spa for this evening; but before that, I kinda just wanted to lay out in the sun and read."

"We can do that. How 'bout we shower first?"

"You broke me. So if you want me to move, you're going to have to do all the work."

"I can do that." I laugh, sitting up. I pull her legs around my waist and carry her into the bathroom.

~~*

"Hell no," I mumble, walking out of the water towards Liz. She's been laying out since we came down to the beach, her white bikini making her already golden skin look darker. She is always hot, but Liz in a bikini under the Caribbean sun, her skin shimmering from the suntan oil she used, her long hair braided down one side of her chest...is perfection. That's not what has my teeth clenching; it's the surfer dude who has pulled his chair up next to hers, trying to get her attention. Lucky for her, she hasn't noticed. As usual, when she has her Kindle in her hand, the world could crumble around her and she wouldn't have a clue. I'm 20 feet away when surfer dude leans over, talking quietly to her. She looks over at him and smiles. My blood starts to boil, making me pick up my pace. I cover the distance between us just as surfer dude says something, making her laugh. All I can think is *that smile is mine; that laugh is mine.* When I reach her, I stand at the end of her lounger; the guy looks up, and Liz bites her lip.

"Do you need something?" surfer dude asks. I don't even look at him.

"Let's go." I take her hand, helping her up.

"Trevor." I can hear the warning in her tone. I ignore it, take her bag from her, take her hand, and walk away from the beach and surfer dude. I do not know what's wrong with me. I have been feeling over-the-top crazy-jealous, crazy-possessive, and just plain fucking crazy. I don't like feeling like this; in fact, I hate it. If she would let me tattoo my name across her forehead, I would consider doing it. Part of me knows that one of the reasons I'm so on edge is because I need to tell her that I love her. The words have been consuming me, eating me alive. I need her to know how I feel, so that I can take the next step and ask her to be my wife. I know people are going to say that we're moving too fast, and we don't know each other, but I don't care. I love her. I get her. I want her to be my forever. Fuck what everyone else says; as long as she will have me, they can all suck it. "Hey, slow down," she says, and I do immediately. We walk silently up to the room, and once we're there, I throw her bag onto the chair, and start pacing back and forth, running my hands over my face and head. "You're freaking me out," she says quietly. I look at her, and before I can think, I'm pushing her towards the bed. Once she's down, I trap her arms above her head. "Trevor, stop. You're scaring me." Her voice wobbles, making me crack.

"I love you."

Finally, the words are out and I feel like I can breathe. "I fucking love you so fucking much that it's making me fucking crazy." I lay my forehead against hers. "I need you to say you will marry me. And don't tell me that it's too soon; I don't give a fuck what anyone says. It's going to happen one way or another, so just agree."

"What?" she questions and I can hear the shock and disbelief in her voice.

"Tell me you love me," I growl. "I'm going fucking crazy; tell me you love me."

"I love you." I watch as tears start to slide into her hair.

Seeing her tears, I realize that I have been such a dick. I hate seeing her cry. "God, baby. I'm so sorry. I'm an asshole. I just needed you to know that I love you, and I want you to be my wife." Great, now I'm sounding like a pussy. I stand, picking her up, and I walk out to the balcony, where I sit down on the couch with her in my lap.

"That has to be the worst proposal in the history of proposals," she says, her face tucked into my neck.

"It's original."

"Yeah," she agrees, but doesn't sound angry. But I'm pissed at myself. In my head, that's not how I ever imagined asking her, and she deserves a lot more than some fucked up jealousy proposal. I don't even have a ring to slide on her finger.

"I take it back."

"What?" she asks, lifting her head and looking at me.

"I take it back. Just forget the whole thing ever happened."

"I—" she starts to talk, but I cut her off when I see tears in her eyes again.

"Shit. No, not that part. Definitely remember the part where I told you I love you; that hasn't changed."

"Oh." Her face scrunches in confusion.

"One day, I'm going to ask you to marry me, and I'll do it the right way. Until then, know that I love you." I run my fingers down her cheek, watching her smile, feeling the weight that has been sitting on my chest finally release.

I lean in and start kissing her. She smells like coconut, ocean, and sun. She leans her head to the side, giving me better access to her neck. Then she's gone, running back into the room. "Shit! I'm late," she says, pulling a dress out of her bag, slipping it on over her head.

"Late for what?"

"I was supposed to meet Mom at the spa twenty minutes ago." She pulls out her hair tie, unravels her braid, then pulls all her hair up into some kind of crazy ball at the top of her head. "I'll be back in a couple hours," she says, picking up her bag from the chair. Before she can run out the door, I grab her, kissing her deeply.

"I love you," I whisper against her lips. She smiles, bending back against my arm, and looks up at me.

"I love you, too." Before I know it, she's gone, the door closing behind her.

"Shit." I rub my face, thinking that I need to call November and see what she thinks I should do about proposing. I flop down on the bed, pull my cell out, and dial her number.

"You're calling me from Jamaica? What's wrong?" November answers on the first ring. I laugh at the motherly tone in her voice, then I hear my niece July start to cry in the background.

"Is this a bad time?" I hear Asher in the background telling her that he'll take care of July while she's on the phone.

"No, your brother's got her. It's his fault anyways; he won't ever put her down, so now, if someone's not holding her, she starts to cry."

"I think you're both to blame for that one."

"Nope, it's all his fault." I can actually feel the love she has for my brother in her voice—as crazy as it sounds. "So what's wrong? Why are you calling me from sunny Jamaica?"

"I think I fucked up."

"Trevor!" she huffs out, sounding just like Mom.

"I didn't fuck up like that."

"How?"

"I told Liz I love her." I don't tell her that I held her down to tell her, then forced her to say it back, then told her she is going to marry me.

"So? She loves you; what's the big deal?"

"How do you know?" I sit up, waiting for her to tell me how she knows. I never wanted Liz to tell me she loved me until she was ready. I didn't want to force her, but that's exactly what I did, held her down and forced her to tell me.

"She told me," November says in a duh-tone, the same one she uses with all of us boys when she thinks were being stupid.

"Why would she tell you and not me?" Now, I'm pissed that she's felt the same way I have and has never said anything, while I've been stewing over this for the last few weeks.

"She wanted to make sure you were both in the same place before she told you."

"Jesus, why do women do that? Why do you guys think that you know what we're thinking?"

"You're a guy; you think about sex and sports. It's not hard to figure out." She laughs right before I hear a loud smack. "Asher," she says, then I hear the phone go quite, and a loud moan. I hang up before I can hear anything else. Listening to my brother have sex with someone who I consider a sister is never going to happen. I lay back on the bed, closing my eyes.

I wake to the sound of someone banging on the door. I look over at the clock; I've been asleep for about two hours. "Coming!" I yell. I don't even look to see who it is; I just open the door, still half asleep. I'm caught off guard when I'm slammed into the wall by my neck.

"What the fuck are you doing with my sister?" Tim asks, his arm planted in my throat. I use my free arm to swing over, switching our positions. He's not expecting the move, judging by the way his body slams into the door.

"Listen to me, you piece of shit," I growl, my hand going around his throat. "I love her, and that's more than I can say for you, the one who had the nerve to steal her money, forcing her to take a second job that just so happened to be working at a fucking strip club." I'm so pissed, I can feel my blood rushing through my veins.

"You have no idea what you're talking about," he coughs out when I loosen the hand around his neck.

"I don't know what I'm talking about? I'm the one she cries to," I retighten my hold around his neck. "Don't tell me I don't know what I'm talking about."

"I didn't have a choice. I need the money. I found out that Kara was pregnant and had to pay off some debts."

"So you stole from your family?"

"You don't have a kid on the way; you don't understand." I shove away from him, walking into the room.

"You're right. I don't have a kid on the way. But I've got a girl and a family, no way I'd put either of them in the middle of my shit."

"Oh, the great Trevor Mayson is all of a sudden better than everyone."

"You don't know anything about me."

"Oh, but doesn't everyone know about you?"

"Did you really come find me to talk about this shit?" I ask, crossing my arms over my chest. My blood is boiling. If it wasn't for my promise to Liz, his ass would be hanging over the balcony.

"I want to know what you're doing with my sister."

"You don't get to ask that; you don't get to play the role of the big brother."

"I love my mom and sister. You may not believe me, but I do."

"Prove it. Come back to town and earn back the money you owe her."

"I have Kara. I—"

I take a step towards him, cutting him off. "That's your choice; but I'm telling you now, if you push me, I will insist that Liz press charges."

"I can't come back to town right now. I'm working undercover."

I shake my head in disgust. "That lie might work on your mom, but it's not working on me. "

"Fuck you," he shouts, his face turning red.

"How long are you going to keep that lie up for?"

"It's not a lie. The people I owed money to trusted me. The cops had no one on the inside, and when they found out about my debt, they offered to pay it off in exchange for me going undercover."

"If they paid off your debt, why did you take the money from your sister?"

"The money I took from her paid the debt; the money the cops gave me paid my interest." I watched him start to pace, his hands running through his shaggy blonde hair. "I had been seeing Kara for a while when she told me she was pregnant." He stops, his eyes meeting mine. "This was around the time that I lost my last bet. I knew I needed to get out from under the people I owed; no way was I going to have a kid and have to look over my shoulder."

"So you took the money, started working for the cops, asked Kara to marry you, and went on your merry way. All the while, your sister is staying in the back room of her store after losing her apartment, working for Mike so that she doesn't lose her dream, and you're living it up, not wondering about the damage you left behind?"

"If you're with her, then why the fuck was she working at a fucking strip club?" he yells.

"Me working for Mike had nothing to do with Trevor," Liz says, walking into the room. She sets her bag down on the bed, coming to my side. Her arm goes around the back of my waist.

"How—"

My girl must not be in the mood to listen. "You need to leave, Tim."

"What?" Tim asks, looking at me. Wrong person. I would always side with Liz; even if I liked him, I would still side with her.

"You need to leave," she states, more firmly this time.

"We need to talk."

"The only thing that I want to hear from you right now is that you're coming home to pay off your debt."

"I can't do that right now."

"Well, then, we have nothing to talk about."

"Sis, don't do this," he pleads, his face looking panicked.

"You never took my feelings into consideration when you did what you did to me."

"I want you to have a relationship with your nephew; you can't just cut me out."

I look down at Liz when her nails dig into my side. "That's not fair," she whispers.

"You need to go," I tell Tim, stepping in front of Liz.

"We're not done talking."

"Until you're ready to tell your sister that you're going to pay back the money you owe, I don't think there is anything for you to talk about."

"Tomorrow is the wedding."

"Do you see the look on your sister's face?" I point towards Liz. "I don't like my woman looking like that, so you need to leave. Tomorrow, if she feels like it, then she will find you; if not, then you need to back the fuck off," I say, pushing him towards the door.

"Who do you think you are?" he asks, making me smile. "I'm her man; and as her man, I can do whatever the fuck I want to anyone I perceive as a threat against her."

"I'm her brother," he says, sputtering as I slam the door in his face. When I turn around, I'm surprised to see Liz smiling. I figured she would be pissed that I just kicked her brother out.

"Thank you," she says, throwing herself into my arms.

"For what?"

"For getting rid of him." She tucks her face into my chest, and I pull her small body tighter against mine.

"I will always protect you."

"I know," she says softly, making me squeeze her a little tighter.

"Did you have a good time with you mom?"

"Yeah," she giggles. I pull her face out of my chest so I can see her.

"What's so funny?"

"Nothing," she says, her face turning red.

"What did you do?"

"Nothing," she says again, taking a step back.

"Your face is bright red," I tell her, looking her over. Her hair is the same as when she left, her skin looks smooth, and she smells like lavender. "Did you get a massage?"

"Yes," she replies, looking down at the ground.

"What else did you guys do?"

"Got manicures and pedicures," she mumbles, still not making eye contact. Then a light bulb goes off, and I'm very interested in finding out if my hunch is correct. I step towards her, my hands going to her dress, and I rip it off over her head. "What are you doing?" she screeches, trying to get away; but I have her trapped.

"I want to see for myself what you had done," I tell her, pushing her back until she has no choice but to sit on the edge of the bed. Dropping to my knees, I pull her foot up towards my chest. "I like this color; what is it called?" I ask, inspecting the light pink color of her nail polish.

"Passionate pink," she says, trying to pull her foot out of my hand.

"Passionate pink," I repeat. I kiss the top of her foot, before setting it on my shoulder. I run my cheek down the inside of her calf, then up her thigh. "Your skin is so soft."

"I...I had a body scrub done." Her voice is breathy; I look up and see that her eyes are hooded and dark, and her cheeks are flushed.

I pick up her other foot, setting it on my other shoulder. My hands pull her knees apart, and I run a finger down the center of her panties. Her hips lift slightly. I lean forward, opening my mouth over the thin cotton that's covering her, and bite down slightly, making her moan. "You smell good." I press my tongue in, making her moan louder. "Tell me you want me to eat you." I look up her body; her head is back, eyes closed. My cock is begging me to pull her down and impale her, but I want her taste on my tongue. "Say 'Trevor, please eat my pussy'." Her eyes open, and she looks at my mouth. Then I bite down again, making her squirm.

· "Trevor, please."

I run my finger along the edge of her panties and dip in slightly, feeling her smooth skin, knowing I was right. "Say it. Say 'Trevor, please eat my pussy'," I growl.

"Trevor, please eat—"

I don't even let her finish. I slide her panties to the side and attack her, licking, biting, and devouring her. "So sweet," I mumble against her. Her hips raise, and her fingers dig into my scalp.

"More," she whimpers, circling her hips.

"My greedy girl," I mumble against her, sliding two fingers deep inside her tightness.

"Trevor!" she screams, her pussy convulsing around my fingers. Her feet try to push me away, but I hold her tighter, wrapping my arms around her thighs, and keeping her in place.

"Stop!" she cries.

"No. Give me another one." I lick her, circling her clit, then sucking deep. Her hips buck, trying to get free. I pull her harder against my mouth, my tongue moving faster until she comes, screaming. I crawl up the bed and pull her body against mine.

"There is nothing more beautiful than watching your body being taken over by what I'm doing to you," I say, sliding between her legs. Her hands go up the front of my shirt, sliding down to the waistband of my shorts. I sit back on my knees, pulling my shirt off over my head. She sits up, unbuttoning my shorts, and tugging them down my hips, her mouth against my abs.

"I love that you're so hard and smooth at the same time," she says, her hands traveling over every inch of skin she can get her hands on.

"I have something else for you that's hard and smooth," I tell her, making her flop back against the bed laughing. "You don't want it?" I ask, smiling. I love that I can laugh with her during sex. I grab my cock, sliding the tip through her pussy. I bite back a groan when I feel her wetness against me. She uncovers her face, and I lean forward to kiss her, nibbling her lips, her tongue touching mine. Her nails dig into my sides, pulling me forward until I slide inside. "Jesus," I say against her mouth, pushing the rest of the way in.

"Yes," she hisses when I feel myself touch her cervix. I don't want to hurt her, but I swear, she loves that shit.

"Who does this tight little pussy belong to?" I swivel my hips, picking up speed.

"You! Oh God! Don't stop," she cries.

"Easy, baby. I lick up her neck. "I love the way you taste." I feel her tighten around me at my words. I bend my head forward, taking her nipple into my mouth and tugging with my lips. "Tell me you love it when I'm inside of you."

"I *love* it when you're inside of me," she moans. Her legs wrap around me, her hips meeting mine as I lift one foot up onto my shoulder, spreading her out, watching myself disappear inside of her. "Oh! Right there; don't stop." She lifts her hips, using my shoulder as leverage. Right before I feel her come around me, her eyes focus on mine; her bottom lip is caught between her teeth. A few more strokes and I follow behind her, groaning her name against her lips. I flip us over so she lands on top of me, running my hands down the smooth skin of her back. After a few sated minutes, she whispers, "I'm sorry about my brother."

"Don't be. I'm sorry that you have to deal with him at all."

"I hope that he's okay. Kara seems sweet; she was at the spa with us, and I really like her. I hope he doesn't get her mixed up in anything."

"Me too, baby."

"Do you think he's telling the truth about what he said?"

The truth is I do believe him. I don't know why he made the stupid decisions that he did, but I believe that he is really working undercover for the cops now. "Yeah, I do believe him. I don't know what happened to get him to this point, but I do believe what he's saying about working for the cops."

"Me too," she whispers. I look out over the water, listen to her breathing even out, and I eventually fall asleep, still in my piece of heaven.

~~*

"I'm so happy that you came with Liz," Rita says, resting her hands on my shoulders. I look across the dance floor to see Liz dancing with George.

"There is nowhere else I would want to be," I tell her mom truthfully. My girl looks beautiful today. Her hair is all up, with small pieces braided throughout, and tied in some kind of knot to the side of her head. Her dress is strapless, and hugs her breasts and waist. The color is a dark green, bringing out the color of her eyes.

"She loves you," Rita says, watching Liz and George dance.

"I know." I smile. I know it's cocky, but who fucking cares? Rita starts laughing, her face going into my chest, just like her daughter's does when she laughs.

"I can see she has her work cut out for her." She looks up at me smiling.

"I love her too, more than I even thought possible," I tell her mom.

"I'm glad she has you." Tears start filling her eyes. "When John died, she took it hard. They were so close; she was a daddy's girl from the day we found out we were having a little girl. Her dad would lay with his face on my stomach, telling her stories. When we brought her home from the hospital, she wasn't happy unless he was holding her. Even as she got older, if he was going somewhere, she wanted to be with him. I know I messed up with her and Tim, but I was so lost in my own grief that I had a hard time seeing that there were other people who were missing him as much as I was. I didn't realize how badly I messed up until the day of her graduation," she says, looking across the room at Liz, who's still dancing with George, smiling up at him. "I had been depressed all morning, thinking about John missing out on one more thing that he would have loved to be a part of. So that morning, I decided that I was going to do something I never did, and went to his grave. When I got to the cemetery, Liz was there in her cap and gown, laying in the grass on top of his grave. I knew then that she must have spent a lot of time there. That's when I realized that I needed to pull my head out of my ass and fight for my daughter, who was just as lost without her father as I was without my husband. I know I will never completely get over losing him, but every day it becomes a little easier, and my heart fills with a little more light. George is wonderful, and I'm blessed to have had two men who have loved me so completely, even with all of my faults," she says, just as George starts walking towards us with Liz.

"Hey, baby," I say, holding out my hand towards Liz.

"Hi." Her smile is shy. She leans up to kiss George's cheek and whispers something in his ear; he smiles and pats my back, takes his new wife from my side, and leads her out onto the dance floor.

"Did you have a good dance?" I pull her into my arms, tucking her head under my chin.

"Yeah, it was very sweet," Liz says, as we sway slowly to the music.

"Good," I say, my lips at the top of her head. I look around when I feel someone watching us. That's when I see Tim on the other side of the dance floor with Kara.

"How about you have a dance with your brother?" I ask.

"Why?"

"I can tell he misses you. And I know you miss him."

"I don't know." She bites her lip, looking across the room to where her brother is dancing.

"I'm right here if you need me; just rub your ear and I will come over to save you."

"Okay," she laughs, looking up at me.

"Okay." I kiss her forehead, leading her towards Tim. When we get to where he's dancing with Kara, he stops and whispers something into Kara's ear. She smiles at Liz, and then walks off towards the restrooms.

"Can we dance?" Liz asks Tim. He nods his head, taking her hand, and leading her out onto the dance floor. I watch as he says something to her. She looks at me smiling, then back at Tim, who looks at me, giving a chin lift. I stand off to the side watching Liz. Kara comes to stand next to me.

"Tim told me some of the stuff that's going on. Thank you for giving him that." She nods towards the dance floor. "I know he messed up, and he knows he did too. We talked, and he wants to move closer to his mom and sister. I don't have any family, so it would be good to have people around when the baby gets here."

"Liz would like that."

"He's going to talk to the detectives that he's working with and see if they can make a bust with the information he has gotten so far." I think about November and July, knowing that Asher would kill himself if something ever happened to them because of something he did.

I turn towards her, watching her closely. "If you want to come to town and stay with us until things get sorted out with him, I think it might be wise for you and the baby," I tell her, looking down at her round stomach.

Her hand rubs her belly, looking down. When her eyes meet mine again, I can see tears in them. "I might take you up on that offer. I don't want to be away from him, but the people that he is dealing with scare me. They know where we live and that I'm pregnant. Tim keeps telling me that things are going to be okay, but I can't get rid of the feeling that something bad is going to happen."

"I'll have Liz talk to him and see if she can help change his mind." I say confidently. She smiles, looking across the room.

"You know, when she told him that the two of you were together, he freaked out about it. He ranted for an hour about you and your history with women." She looks at me and smiles. "I can see that you really love her; I think that he sees that now, too."

"More than anything," I confirm, watching Liz walk towards me holding Tim's hand. Just as she reaches my side, George picks Rita up, announcing he and his new bride are retiring for the evening. They leave the room with hoots and hollers following behind them. I smile at Liz, whose face has turned bright red.

"Let's all have a drink and talk," I say, looking at our group. The rest of the evening is spent talking and laughing. The next day, when we head home,

I know that I need to find a way to put a ring on Liz's finger, and make her mine permanently.

Chapter 8

Liz

It's been two months since we got back from Jamaica. Two months of heaven. The week after we got home, I officially moved in with Trevor. I would love to say that he wasn't his normal bossy self when he asked me to live with him, but sadly, he was himself. I had been at the house all day with Lolly. I cleaned and did laundry, and when Trevor came home with his work clothes covered with mud, his boots leaving muddy prints all over my freshly mopped floor, I was pissed. So I told him that he should've taken off his stuff before tracking mud into the house. He told me I didn't have a right to bitch about it because I didn't live with him. So I told him if that's how he felt, then I was never going to live with him, and that I should move back to Mike's. When I said that, he threw the beer that he'd just opened across the room, where it exploded against the wall. He yelled that he didn't know why I wouldn't unpack my bag and put my shit away, when I acted like we were living together.

That was about the time I picked my purse up off the table, and left to stay the night at Mike's. Well, I *tried* to stay at Mike's. It was about three o'clock in the morning when I was picked up and carried to Trevor's truck. He didn't say anything except, "Can't sleep." When we got back home, he tucked me under his big body, kissed my hair, and fell asleep. In the morning, when we woke up, he apologized for acting like a jerk, and said that he hated seeing my bag tucked under his bed; it made him feel like I could easily leave without much effort. Then he proceeded to slide inside me, his mouth over mine when he asked me if I would move in.

Now, you tell me, if Trevor Mayson was inside you, asking you to live with him, what would you do? Exactly. You would no doubt move in without a second thought, especially as he's thrusting inside you, telling you how much you mean to him and that he loves you.

Since I moved in, we started to renovate the kitchen. The first thing we did was knock down the wall in-between the kitchen and living room. The next step was taking down all the old cabinets. Then we went to Alabama for the night so that we could go to Ikea and pick out a whole new kitchen. We chose white cabinets with a large country sink, stainless steel appliances, and his friend who works with concrete did painted concrete countertops that looked amazing with the bright, multi-colored back splash that we chose. I have been feeling like I'm living a dream, waking up to the man that I love every day. The only thing that nags me is that he hasn't brought up proposing again since Jamaica. I know that he said to forget it, but I can't; I keep wondering why he told me to forget, or that he said anything about it. I want to be Elizabeth Star Mayson more than anything. I talked to November about it, and she said that I shouldn't stress, and that she's sure that he loves me, but wants to make sure that the timing is right to ask me to be his wife. I don't know what to think at this point. The other day, I caught him counting my birth control pills when I walked into the kitchen. When I told him that I was taking them and not to worry about it, he got a funny look on his face, pulled me to him, and kissed me silly.

"You about ready?" Trevor says, coming up behind me, dragging me out of my thoughts. He has on a black, long-sleeved t-shirt, with his dark jeans and work boots. We're meeting up with everyone at the bar to play a few games of pool. November and Asher are even meeting us there. Asher's parents, Susan and James, are watching July for the night so that we can all hang out.

"Yeah, just give me, like, fifteen minutes. I need to get my clothes on." His arms wrap around me, his mouth nuzzling my neck.

"Tomorrow, I'm taking you somewhere," he says against the skin of my neck. I tilt my head, giving him more room, my eyes closing against the feeling his mouth creates.

"Where?" I breathe deep, trying to prevent the moan from climbing up my throat.

"You'll see when we get there." He smiles, his eyes meeting mine in the mirror. He looks so happy that I wonder what he's up to. "Now, let's go before I pull down those tiny shorts you've got on, and slide into your pussy, making you watch in the mirror while I fuck you." I bite my lip, thinking that I wouldn't mind at all if he wanted to do that. In fact, I would be perfectly happy with that option. He starts laughing, his fingers digging into my hips. "Later, I'm going to fuck you right here. I will be hard all night thinking about the things I'm going to do to you while you watch." He turns me around, taking my hand and placing it over his very hard, very large erection that is pushing the limits of his zipper. My breathing picks up. I can feel the rapid pulse in my clit. "Later," he says against my mouth, before I feel his tongue against mine. The kiss is so hot that I don't want to go anywhere; I want him now. He takes my arms from around his neck, kisses my forehead, and leaves the bathroom. "Come on, baby. We gotta go; get a move on," he yells from somewhere in the house.

"Hold your horses; I'm coming!" I yell back, going into the bedroom to pull on my jeans and a cardigan. All the while, thinking about where he may be taking me tomorrow.

~~*

"Oh, look who it is," Jen says, with Britney and Cindy standing on each side of her. I ignore them and walk to the sink to wash my hands. "Look I'm going to be a friend an—"

"Oh, great." I roll my eyes, cutting her off before she can say anything else. I look at the three of them in the mirror, my eyes landing on Jen. "I had a feeling we couldn't just skip this part." I look over my shoulder at all three of the girls standing there. "I knew this was coming at some point tonight; I just didn't know when," I say. Since we got to the bar, Jen has been trying to get Trevor's attention. She took off her sweater, leaving her in a white tank top and a very-apparent red lace bra. She walked by the table a few times, and then tried flirting with Cash. This didn't work, I guess. Cash has been seeing some girl he met when he and Trevor went to Alabama. He has been spending most of his free time there with her. Then she tried to talk to Nico, who promptly told her that he didn't want to fuck her, so she should move on. Now, this. I knew it was coming; I just didn't know when.

"What are you talking about?" Jen asks, looking confused.

"You know, the part that's in every movie and every book ever written; the one where you tell me that Trevor doesn't care about me, and is only using me for sex...blah, blah, blah." I narrow my eyes at her.

"It's true; he doesn't care about you." She flips her long red hair over her shoulder. "I'm just trying to save you the heartache." She pouts out her bottom lip.

"Awww, that so sweet. But I think I'll stick around for a while. I mean, Lord, the things that man can do in bed are mind blowing. There's this trick he does, when he's going to—"

"You bitch! Stay away from him," Jen yells, taking a step towards me.

"You should tell *Trevor* to stay away from *me*," I smirk. I know she has tried to do that before and got shut down in front of all of her friends. I hate when women act desperate when it comes to men who don't want them. Sadly, Jen is beautiful and could probably get any man she wanted if she wasn't a whack job, as Trevor so eloquently put it.

"I'm telling—"

"You okay, baby?" Trevor asks, sticking his head into the bathroom. Nico pushes the door open all the way, stepping inside.

"Fuck yeah! Party in the bathroom!" Nico yells, making me laugh. I look at Jen, who is trying to kill me with her eyes. Trevor leans in, grabbing my hand pulling me out into the hall, where he presses me against the wall, trapping me with his weight.

"You good?" he asks, leaning in so that his mouth is next to my ear. I can't focus when his body is pressed so tightly against mine.

"I'm okay," I tell him, looking over his shoulder at Jen, who is walking out of the bathroom. Her eyes meet mine, and I know she's not done with whatever evil plan she's cooking up. "You're right; she is a bitch," I tell Trevor, making him laugh.

"If she fucks with you again, tell me. I knew she was up to something when I saw her and her posse walking into the bathroom after you left the table."

"She said she wanted to give me some friendly advice, and that I should stay away from you," I tell him matter-of-factly.

"That was nice of her." Trevor smiles.

"I know. But I told her that I couldn't break up with you yet because you're good in bed. Then I was going to tell her about the thing you do with your tongue when you're going down on me, but you showed up."

"Sorry to have ruined your shining moment," he laughs.

"You should be sorry." I push at his chest. "I was going to verbally kick her ass."

"Poor baby." He laughs harder, kissing the side of my neck.

"When we get home, I'll rub your ego to make up for the interruption."

"I'm sure you will," I smile.

He grabs my face, holding it between his hands. "I love you. Don't ever doubt that you're the best thing that has ever happened to me."

"Do not make me cry in the middle of the bar, Trevor Earl Mayson."

He looks up, his eyes bugging out. "Your mom told me," I shrug.

"If you ever tell anyone my middle name, I will spank you."

"Oh! So scary, *Earl*," I laugh, ducking under his arm and running away from him. Before I can get too far, he has me up and over his shoulder. His hand lands on my ass with a loud smack, making me laugh harder. "You put me down right now, Ea—"

Before I can get the words out, I'm flipped, and his mouth is covering mine.

He pulls his mouth from mine, leaving me breathless. "Now, behave yourself."

I smile up at him, and when I glance around the bar, I notice that Jen and her crew had been watching our little spectacle. I smirk at them and toss my hair over my shoulder. What I really want to do is yell *ha ha he's mine* and stick out my tongue.

"Fine," I say, walking back to the table, noticing that November is drinking cranberry juice.

"Hey, are you okay?" I ask her, looking down at the glass in front of her.

"Oh yeah. I'm fine. I just don't feel like drinking."

"You don't feel like drinking?" I ask, surprised. She always drinks beer when we're out, except when she was—

"We're pregnant." Asher says proudly, puffing out his chest.

"Oh my God! Congrats!" I hug November, and then stand to hug Asher. "When did you find out?"

"This morning." Asher puts his arm around her, kissing her nose.

"When do you find out what you're having?"

"Not for a few weeks," November says, rubbing her belly.

"It's a boy," Asher says, his hand moving to her waist. Trevor starts laughing, along with Cash and Nico. "I made sure to do it on the right side," Asher says deadpan, glaring at his brothers. I start laughing so hard that tears slide down my cheeks.

"We know, honey," November says, patting Asher's chest.

"Well, whatever it ends up being, congrats, guys. That's awesome," Trevor says, hugging November, and then patting his brother on the back. When Trevor looks at me, he smiles, making a knot form in my stomach. The look in his eyes says a lot more than I want to hear. I try to shake myself out of the feeling.

"That's so exciting," I cry, clapping my hands. "Let's have a drink. I mean, you can't drink because you're, you know, but I—um—I'll be back," I sputter out, needing to get away from Trevor and the look on his face.

"Are you okay?" Nico asks, leaning on the bar next to me.

"Yeah," I say, signaling the bartender. When she finally gets to me, I ask for a shot of tequila.

"Tequila?" Nico asks, his eyebrows drawn together.

"Yep." I tip the shot back without salt or lime, then tap the glass, signaling for a refill. I start to lift it to my mouth, when it's taken from my hand from over my shoulder, and given to Nico. "That's mine." I pout as Nico takes my shot.

"We're going home," Trevor says, wrapping an arm around my waist.

"No, I'm spending time with everyone."

"You were, then you ran off; now we're going home."

"Can you *not* be a jerk?"

"We have plans tomorrow morning, so we need to leave anyways."

"I can have Nico drop me off at home if you're leaving," I suggest.

"No, you can't have Nico drop you off at home," Nico says, laughing.

"Fine." I walk back to the table, grabbing my purse. "I guess we're leaving," I tell November, who looks at my face, then at Trevor, and starts laughing.

"That's fine. We need to leave as well," November says, getting off her barstool. "But we will see you this weekend for the party, right?" she asks, looking at me, and I have no idea what she's talking about.

"What party?" I ask, then look around when I notice that everyone has gotten quiet.

"Oh, it's not a party; it's a—um—Bar-B-Que," Asher says, cutting in.

"We'll be there," Trevor says, glaring at everyone before pulling me out the door behind him.

"I didn't know we were going to a Bar-B-Que this weekend," I tell him, as he lifts me up into the truck and buckles me in.

"It slipped my mind," he tells me, kissing my forehead.

"Oh," I say, laying my head on his shoulder, relaxing into his side once he starts the truck. The tequila is making me feel all warm and fuzzy. I'm such a lightweight.

"Why is it that every time someone talks about kids, you panic?"

I sit up; I knew this day was coming. "I told you before, I don't want kids."

"I want kids, Liz, and I know that you do too. I see the longing in your face anytime you hold July, or even when you met Kara and noticed she was pregnant."

I do want them; deep down there is nothing I want more then to be a mother. But I can't do it; I can't have children, and then leave them behind. "I told you before, Trevor, that if that was a deal breaker for you, then you should get out before feelings were involved."

"Tell me that you never want kids."

'I...' I can't say it; the words just won't come out.

"We are going to make beautiful babies, and you are going to be an awesome mom," he says, kissing the top of my head. My stomach is in knots, my palms sweating. I want to tell him so badly that I don't want kids, but I can't. When I think about having a little boy, with big brown eyes and long dark lashes, who looks just like Trevor, I can't tell him that I don't want that. I lay my head back on his shoulder, clearing my mind of everything except the alcohol coursing through my system. When we finally pull up to the house, I go straight to the bathroom, change into pajamas, and get into bed. When I'm almost asleep, Trevor gets into bed, tucking me under him like he always does. I feel him kiss the top of my head, and hear him tell me he loves me, right before I fall asleep.

~~*

"Tell me again why I have to wear a blindfold?" I ask Trevor, who is carrying me somewhere. I had gotten up this morning, alone in the house. At first, I thought he was mad about last night and decided to cut his losses, but then I wandered into the kitchen and there was a pot of coffee waiting for me, along with a note telling me that he had gone for a run. I was on my second cup of coffee when he came into the house, his white t-shirt plastered to his body with sweat. He was pulling it off as he walked into the kitchen, without realizing that I was there, unaware that he was putting on a show.

I watched as he wiped his head, face, and then his chest without looking up. His baggy sweats hung so low on his hips that if you pulled down slightly, you would get the full experience of Trevor Mayson. When he lifted his head and his eyes caught mine, he smirked. Walking towards me, he kissed my forehead, and went to the laundry room, where I could hear him banging around, most likely destroying some innocent piece of clothing. The other day, he called and asked me if he could wash towels with other laundry. I told him yes, thinking he would know to still separate the dark and lights. Oh, was I wrong. He washed a red towel with the white laundry, turning all the white t-shirts he wears to work a nice light pink.

"Morning," he said, walking back into the kitchen.

"Morning," I replied, looking at his abs as he moved around, pulling things from the cupboards. I had no idea what kind of work went into looking like he does, but seriously, I loved looking at him.

"Stop looking at me like that, you little pervert," he said, laughing and making my face heat.

"Stop walking around half naked," I mumbled into my coffee cup, still looking over the rim at his body.

"Nah," he said, shaking his head. "I like that look." He kissed my head. "We need to leave in about an hour; be ready to go," he told me, leaning against the counter to eat a bowl of cereal.

I glared at him, but agreed with an "okay." I grabbed a banana off the counter. Peeling it, I slid it into my mouth, looking at him, watching his eyes darken, and then I took a big bite, and made sure that my teeth made a loud chomping sound.

"Ouch!" he laughed, covering himself with his hand. I smirked at him over my shoulder, walking out of the kitchen.

"Yes, you need the blindfold," he tells me, bringing me back to the present. He's holding me closer. I know we're outside; I can smell flowers and feel the sun beating down on me. "I'm going to stand you up now," he says, lowering me to the ground. I hold onto his shoulders, and as my feet touch the ground, my stomach fills with butterflies, and my pulse kicks up. "This is our first stop," he tells me, taking off my blindfold. I look around seeing that we're in the cemetery where my father is buried. My stomach drops when I look down at my dad's grave.

"Why are we here?" I ask, looking at Trevor, who is now looking nervous.

"I wanted to meet him. You don't talk to me about him very often, and I know that he was important to you."

I nod in agreement. "He was my best friend," I tell him, looking at my dad's headstone. "No matter what happened, I knew that I could talk to him about anything, and he would listen. Or if I had a problem, he would help me find a solution."

"He sounds like he was a good man," he says, wrapping his arms around me.

"He was the best; he would have liked you," I reply, and tears start falling from my eyes.

"I would have liked him too." He holds my face in his hands, kissing each eye. "He's one of the reasons why you are so beautiful on the inside, along with the outside. He's one of the reasons I couldn't help but fall in love with you."

I sob, my head crashing into his chest; he holds me for a long time, just standing outside with the breeze blowing, and the sun beating down on us. When I finally calm down, he asks me to go wait in the truck, and says that he would be with me in a few minutes. I kneel down on the ground in front of my dad's headstone and send him a silent message telling him that I am happy, and that I love and miss him. Then I stand up, kiss Trevor, and walk back to the truck to wait for him.

I watch him from the passenger seat as he too kneels down in front of Dad's headstone. I can see his lips moving, but can't make out the words. But then, he reaches out, pats the top of the headstone, stands up, and makes his way to the driver's side of the truck.

Once back in the truck, he takes the blindfold out of his pocket, wrapping it back over my eyes. "One more stop," he says. I feel the truck reverse, and we drive for a good while. When he parks the truck, he drags me out on his side, carrying me again, but this time, just a short ways. When he stops walking, he sets me on the ground, leads me by my hand, and helps me sit; I can tell it's a swing I'm sitting on. When he removes the blindfold, he's kneeling in front of me. I look around to see where we are.

"Why are we here?" I tilt my head back, looking up at the tree I was sitting under. The swing is one I used to swing on all the time when I was young. The old rope ties up high in the branches of the old giant weeping willow; the outer branches of the tree creates its own private escape for whoever was swinging.

"I talked to your mom, and she told me that the two of them would spend time here when they were dating. She also told me that this is where your dad asked her to marry him." His eyes are warm when he's talking about my parents.

"It is; this was my dad's favorite spot," I tell him, remembering coming here when I was little. "I used to make my dad push me on this swing for hours. Sometimes he would bring a picnic; once, he even had a tea party here with me and dressed up." I laugh, and so does Trevor.

When he looks over my face, I see so much love in his eyes that my palms start to sweat and I hold my breath. "Your mom told me that this was a special place for you, a spot full of love and happiness. That's why I wanted to bring you here."

"Oh," I say, watching Trevor lean forward and pull something out of his pocket, before returning to his kneeling position.

"You are my best friend. I can laugh with you—and fight with you—but I always know that I will be with you. You are the person I want to start a family with, grow old with, make memories with, dream with, cry with, and live this life with. Will you marry me?" He holds the ring out to me between two fingers. I cover my mouth, looking down at the beautiful ring with an emerald-cut stone my eyes shoot up to his. "This is the part where you say, 'I can't imagine living my life without you'...and say yes." He actually looks nervous.

"Yes," I struggle to get out with my mouth still covered. He takes the hand that's covering my mouth, brings it to his, and kisses my fingers, before sliding the ring on.

"Perfect," he says, kissing my finger before pulling me down to him.

"This has to be the best proposal in the history of proposals," I tell him, laughing.

"I figured I fucked up the first one pretty badly; I needed to make up for that."

"The first proposal was you," I tell him, pulling my face away from his neck so I can look at him. "You're very bossy and demanding; that's one of the reasons I love you."

"You're stuck with me for life."

"I know; maybe I'm crazy, but that makes me very happy." I laugh when he starts tickling me.

"Let's go home crazy girl."

"Let's go home and celebrate," I clarify.

"Oh, we're definitely going to celebrate." He picks me up, tosses me over his shoulder, and walks us back up to the truck.

On the ride home, I ask him what he was saying when he was alone for those few minutes at my dad's grave. He tells me that he was asking Dad's permission to ask me to marry him. I didn't think I could fall any more in love with Trevor, but apparently, I was very wrong. My heart swells with love for my fiancé—wow...my *fiancé*—and when we got home, we celebrated all night long.

Chapter 9

Trevor

The night after the "bar-b-que"—, which was really a surprise engagement party—I flip on the bedside lamp when I hear the phone ring. "Yeah?" I answer, when I see Cash's number on the display.

"Meet me at the barn in twenty," he says, before he hangs up. I look down at the phone in my hand, wondering what the hell is going on. Since we were kids, if one of us has a problem, we meet at the old barn on my parents' property. I look down at Liz, who is sleeping soundly beside me. Her face is tucked into the crook of my arm, her breathing even, and her hand with her engagement ring laying across my abs.

"Baby," I whisper, running my fingers down her smooth cheek.

"Go away," she mumbles, smacking at my hand. I chuckle, running my hand down her cheek again, making her swat at me, before rolling away from me. "Baby," I say again, this time near her ear, making her groan and hide her head under the pillow. "I need to leave; I'll be back," I say. Her head comes out from under the pillow, and she looks at the clock, then me.

"It's three in the morning." Her voice is soft, her eyes sleepy and concerned.

"Cash called, and he needs me."

"Is he okay?" She sits up, her white tank top hiding nothing. "Should I come with you?" she asks, pulling her hair out of her face, looking around the room, adorably confused.

"No. Go back to sleep."

"Are you sure?" she asks, as I tuck her back into bed.

"I'm sure," I say, kissing her before I pull on a pair of jeans and a t-shirt. I walk back over to my side of the bed, where Liz has cuddled down into the blankets, and kiss her forehead, telling her I love her.

"Lolly," I call into the living room. Lolly comes down the hallway wagging her tail, thinking that it's time for breakfast. "Come lay down." I point to the floor near the door, knowing that if I'm gone, she will stay and look after my girl. I walk into the living room, grab my boots and pulling them on, grab my keys from the bowl Liz had placed near the door, lock up the house behind me, and head out to my truck.

"What's going on?" I ask as soon as I walk into the large old barn. The inside is separated into two levels. The top is an old hayloft, and the bottom is an empty space except for an old card table, with a few chairs gathered around it.

"Waiting until Asher gets here, then I'll explain," Cash says, pacing back and forth, running his hands down the back of his neck.

"Do you know what's going on?" I ask Nico, who's sitting in one of the chairs watching Cash pace.

"No clue." He shrugs, and I sit in the chair next to him, watching Cash, becoming more concerned by the second. When Asher walks in, Nico and I stand.

"What's going on?" Asher asks, looking at Cash. And for the first time in my life, I watch my normally-happy little brother break down. Cash's head falls forward as we all gather around him. I put my hand on Cash's shoulder, and when his eyes come up, he runs his hands down his face.

"I fucked up," Cash says, his voice broken.

"Whatever it is, we will figure it out; tell us what's going on."

"Jules is pregnant. How the fuck am I going to fix that?" he asks, his eyes pleading.

"Jesus," I mumble, running my hands down my face, before looking at all three of my brothers.

"I thought you were with Lilly?" Nico asks. I'm sure we're all wondering. Cash has been all about Lilly since he met her and we got back from Alabama; if he has the weekend off, he spends it with her near her school. He was even thinking about asking her to transfer schools so that she could be closer.

"I broke it off with her," he says, looking away.

"Dude, are you sure that she's even pregnant? Or even if she is, you sure that it's your kid?" Nico asks for all of us again.

"I went to the doctor with her today, and the doctor confirmed that around the time I slept with her is when she had gotten pregnant."

"What the fuck?" Nico looks at me, and I know exactly what he's thinking.

"Did you use protection?" I ask.

"Yeah! I'm not stupid." He groans. "We had been hooking up for a while but we both agreed that's all it was ever going to be."

"Did you have the condom, or did she?"

"Does it fucking matter whose condom we used?"

"I fucking told you that Jules was telling people at the bonfire that she wanted to get knocked up. Do you remember that conversation, dumbass?"

"I slept with her before you told me that shit!" he roars, throwing the card table across the room. "I haven't slept with anyone else since I met Lilly."

"Shit," I whisper.

"Calm down," Asher says, taking a step toward him. "You know that no matter what, we will be here for you, whatever you need."

"I just broke up with my girl." Cash looks at me, pleading. "I didn't want her to have to go through this with me, so I called her and broke it off with her over the phone. I didn't even have the balls to break it off with her in person."

"You didn't have to do that," Asher says.

"Jules is pregnant with my child. After I saw my son and heard his heartbeat today, I knew what I had to do. I can't be so selfish as to think that Lilly would want to stick with me through this, knowing that I'm having a child with another woman." I didn't like that he was going through this, but I understood why he would feel conflicted about having Lilly in this situation.

"Look I understand what you're going through," Asher says, rubbing the back of his head. "You're a good man, Cash. And out of all of us, you wear your heart on your sleeve; you always have. We need to make sure that this is your kid."

"I know he's mine; I feel it in my gut."

"Okay, so what do you need from us?" Nico asks.

"I'm going to tell mom and dad in the morning. I need you guys to be there. Jules has been living with her aunt, and I'm going to have her move in with me so that if she needs anything, I'm close by."

"I don't think that's a good idea." Asher looks at me for back up.

"You asked me what I need, and I need your support. I need to know that you got my back."

"We got your back," we all say in unison. "No matter what happens, you have us," I tell him. Asher and Nico nod in agreement.

"How 'bout I get the six-pack I have in my truck, and we all have a beer. Dad will be up in an hour to go down to the station; we can just head over there this morning," Nico says.

"Sounds good to me," I agree, looking at Asher.

"Works for me. I fed July before I left the house; my girls should be sleeping for a while."

"I need a couple beers," Cash says, sitting down in one of the chairs, his elbows to his knees, and his head hung low. I watch Asher and Nico head outside before I walk to where Cash is.

"It will be alright," I tell him, sitting in a chair next to him.

"Lilly's my one," he whispers so low that I barely hear him. His hands cover his face, and then come to rest over his mouth when our eyes connect.

"Fuck," I say, leaning my head back. I can't imagine having to give up Liz.

"Yeah," he agrees, before looking at the door and watching Asher walk in with Nico close behind.

It is after ten in the morning when I walk into my house. The house is quiet, so I walk back to the bedroom and can hear the shower in the master bath going. When I open the bathroom door, Liz screams as I step into the steam-filled room, pulling my shirt off over my head.

"Trevor?" she asks, wiping some of the fog from the shower door, and holding her chest.

260

"It's me, babe," I confirm, pulling off my boots and jeans.

"I'm just getting out; do you want me to leave the water on for you?" Liz asks, as I look at her through the fog-covered glass doors of the shower.

"You step out of that shower, baby, and I'm going to get you dirty. So I suggest you just stay there." After the night and morning I had, feeling Cash's pain over losing the girl that he was falling in love with, I need Liz more than I need my next breath. I need to know that she is here with me, and that she is mine.

She doesn't say anything, just watches me get undressed. When I open the shower door, she takes a step back, making room for me. I pull her into my arms, and rest my head on top of hers. Her arms wrap tighter around my middle as her body relaxes into mine.

"Are you okay?" she asks, leaning her head back to look at me.

"Yeah." Her eyes roam my face.

"Is Cash okay?"

I let out a deep breath before answering, "He will be."

"Do you want to talk about it?" she asks, but I don't want to talk right now.

"No, I want you on your knees." She looks startled, but then she licks her lips, sinking to her knees in front of me. I'm surprised by this move on her part; she must know that I need this, desperate to know that she's mine in every way. My hands go to her hair, holding it away from her face. Running her hands up my thighs, she wraps her small hand around my cock. Her tongue comes out, licking over the head as her hand slides up and down the length. "No teasing; open up." I tell her, and she takes me all the way in, looking up at me; her eyes are dark with lust, her plump lips stretching around my girth. Her rhythm is perfect; my cock touches the back of her throat every time she takes me all the way in. "You have a hot little mouth, baby," I tell her, throwing my head back and enjoying the feel of her mouth wrapped around me.

Her rhythm picks up, and her mouth and hand move faster. When I look back down at her, her other hand has disappeared between her legs. "Does having my dick in your mouth turn you on?" She moans as I run my hand down her cheek. "Stop touching yourself." She hesitates and whimpers, before putting her hand on my thigh. I hold her face, watching myself disappear between her lips a few more times before I start to feel that tingle in my spine. "Stop." I lift her under her arms, standing her up and turning her around. Then I place her hands on the shower wall. My fingers slide over her clit. "You're soaked; you love sucking me off, don't you, baby?"

"Yes," she moans, pressing back and trying to get more contact. I lean forward, sinking my teeth into her shoulder at the same time I slam into her. One arm goes around her waist, my free hand goes between her legs, and I play with her clit.

"Shit, Trevor!" she yells, her hand reaches behind her, going around to grab onto the muscle of my ass to pull me deeper into her. She leans her head to the side, her mouth seeking mine, and our tongues touch. I'm lost in her.

"You're never leaving me." I slam into her, punctuating my words. "You're never getting rid of me. Tell me you want to have my child."

"Yes!" she screams, convulsing around me. Her pussy pulls me in, bringing on my own orgasm. I lay my forehead against her back, trying to catch my breath. I know that it's fucked up to ask her to have my baby when I know she's getting ready to have an orgasm; but fuck, I need her tied to me. "Oh my God! What was that?" she laughs.

"A moment that will be burned into my brain for the rest of my life." I lift my head from her back. Her forehead is resting against her arm on the tile wall. I slide out of her slowly; I hate losing the heat of her. I turn her around, kissing her before burying my face in her neck, absorbing her smell.

"Are you okay?" she asks softly, hugging me a little tighter.

"Yeah, let's get washed up. I'll tell you what's going on while you have some coffee."

"Alright, but give me a second; my legs are still kind of wobbly."

I smile, making her eyes narrow. "Come here. I'll wash you up." I spend quite a bit of time washing her, and then eating her out, before I shut off the water and step out of the shower. I hold out a towel for her to wrap up in before I pull one down for me to dry off. Once we're dressed and in the kitchen, I tell her about Cash and Jules. The more I talk, the more pissed off she becomes.

"So that girl from the bonfire wasn't joking. She seriously wanted to get knocked up by one of you guys?"

I shrug. "I don't know what the hell happened. All I know is that Cash slept with her."

"And he knows it's his?"

"He can't be sure without a paternity test, but he believes that the timing matches how far along she is."

"That's crazy. So what, he dumped Lilly and is moving Jules in with him?"

"That's what he says. Tomorrow we're supposed to help him move her into his house."

"Oh my God." She covers her mouth. "She's getting exactly what she wants, and poor Cash is stuck."

"It's his choice, baby." I tell her softly. "He doesn't want his kid growing up without him."

"He can still see his kid, Trevor!" she practically yells.

"You have to understand, we grew up in a house with both our parents. He wants that for his son." I don't tell her that Cash took me aside and told me that Jules told him that if he didn't do what she wanted that she would get an abortion.

"His son?"

"Yeah, they're having a boy."

"I feel so horrible for him."

"Me too; but who knows? He and Jules could end up happy," I tell her, hoping I'm right.

She shakes her head, looking out the window. "Yeah, I guess you're right."

"Asher is talking to November, and I wanted to talk to you about—"

"You don't even have to say it. I know that Cash is a good guy; and regardless of how I feel about Jules, I will be nice to her."

"Thank you." I walk over, kissing her forehead. "Is your brother still bringing Kara tomorrow?" I ask.

After we got back from Jamaica, Tim called saying that the cops he was working with agreed that the best thing to do is have Kara stay somewhere else while they put the finishing touches on the case against the people Tim was spying on. Tim talked to Mike and explained the situation, and that when it was all said and done, he would come work for me and my brothers to earn the money to pay back what Mike had given to Liz. Tim said that Mike also told him that they could stay in the downstairs apartment, where November and Liz used to live, until they were able to start out on their own. It was a win-win for everyone involved. Tim would pay back the money to Mike. I got a new worker. Liz had someone to help her out in the store, and Kara would have people around to help her out, before and after the baby arrived.

"Yeah, Tim said that he can only stay the night, and then has to go back."

"Well, tomorrow when I'm helping get Jules moved, you can go over and get Kara settled in; then tomorrow night, we can all go out to dinner. How does that sound?"

"Awesome," she smiles, and then looked over my face. "You look exhausted. Why don't you try to sleep for a while?"

"Why don't you take a nap with me?"

"You and I both know that if I get in that bed with you, you're going to try and have your wicked way with me and not get any sleep."

"Hmmm...or you could try to put me to sleep."

"By what, suffocating you with a pillow?" she asks with a mock-glare.

"I thought I mellowed you out with the three orgasms I gave you."

Her cheeks turn pink, making her look adorable. "How can my girl be so dirty, then act so shy when I say the word orgasms?"

"I'm not dirty," she says, offended.

"Oh, baby, you're so dirty that I think we need to take another shower." I say the words close to her ear; I feel her shiver, her hands going to my shoulders, and her nails biting into my skin.

"You're insatiable."

"Only for you."

"You're really good with that mouth of yours, Mr. Mayson."

"I know," I tell her smugly, putting her up on the counter.

"Ugh...I don't mean like that; I mean with words."

"Sure you do." I spread her legs, pulling her ass to the edge. The tank top and panties she's wearing give me easy access.

"I have stuff to do today," she says. At the same time, she leans her head to the side, giving my mouth more access to her neck.

"I'll be quick," I tell her, knowing that I'm not letting her go anywhere. And I don't. We spend the rest of the day in bed, in the kitchen, and in the shower; and in each place, I'm inside of Liz.

~~*

"So, that's it," I say, setting the last box down in the living room.

"Yep," Cash says, looking over at Jules who is in the kitchen.

"You sure about this?" I ask, watching Cash's jaw tick as he watches Jules switch out his stuff for hers.

"No," he says, walking into the kitchen and opening the fridge to grab a beer. Jules says something, making his jaw go tight; then he nods, walking back out into the living room. "Look, thanks for your help today, but I think you guys should go," Cash says, looking at Nico, Asher, and me. "Jules is tired, and I'm fucking exhausted."

"Yeah, sure, send me a text," Nico says, patting Cash's back before he walks out. Asher hugs him, saying something that I can't hear, before turning and walking off.

"If you need anything, call," I tell him, patting his shoulder. He lifts his chin, walking me to the door.

"I'll see you at the site tomorrow," he says, as the door closes behind me. I can't help but to feel like I just left my brother in his own personal hell.

When I get out to my truck, Nico and Asher are standing near the tailgate talking. "What's up?" I look between them.

"She's taking over kind of quickly," Nico says.

"Noticed that, did you?" Asher asks, rubbing the back of his neck. "I don't know about you guys but I hope to god this isn't some fucked up game and that this kid is his."

"We all know Cash wears his heart on his sleeve; he always has," Nico says, shaking his head.

"That's what worries me," Asher grumbles under his breath.

"You did the same thing," I remind him. Wanting to change the subject no one but me knows what Jules told him and it's not my place to spread that shit. Cash is already stressed out about this if everyone knew what she was telling him. I shake my head at my own thoughts.

"I did, and that shit turned out to be a lie. I don't want to see Cash go through that," Asher says. I know he knows how Cash feels. His ex-claimed to be pregnant so that he would marry her, then it turned out she was never even pregnant at all; she made the whole story up so that he would commit to her.

"No matter how we feel about it, he needs our support," I tell them, before looking at the time on my phone. "I need to head out. Liz's brother is in town for the night dropping off his fiancée."

"So when is he going to be here permanently?" Nico asks.

"Not sure," I shrug, pulling my keys out of my pocket.

"Tomorrow, I won't be at the site. I have a job with Kenton," Nico says, looking between Asher and me. "I know that you guys don't want to hear it, but we need to come up with a figure so you can buy me out."

"You're sure that's what you want?" Asher asks.

"I told you guys before, construction is all I've ever known; but tracking people is something I'm good at. I love doing it."

"It's not safe." I say, shaking my head.

"Neither is working on a jobsite; anything can happen when we're building a house."

"True. "Asher nods, shoving his hands in the pockets of his jeans. "If it's what you want to do, find out how much your percentage of the business is worth. We'll all get together, go over the numbers, and figure out how to make it happen."

"I'll let you know," Nico says, walking towards his car. I watch him go, worried about both of my little brothers for different reasons. My phone beeps with a message. I look down reading it.

LIZ: I'm starving. Come feed me.

ME: Be there soon.

I type back the quick response, not even realizing that I have been smiling.

"What's that smile for?" I look up at Asher and glare.

"That's the, I'm-pussy-whipped smile," Nico yells out his car window, before pulling out of the driveway.

Asher laughs, and I flip Nico off. "Gotta go," I say, opening up my truck door.

"See you tomorrow," Asher says, climbing into his Jeep. I give him a flick of my fingers, before starting up my truck and heading home.

~~*

"So how did today go?" I ask Liz, who is sprawled out on top of me. When we got home from dinner with Tim and Kara, I couldn't get her naked and in bed fast enough. Once we finished, she climbed off me, went to the bathroom to clean up, then came back to bed with a rag, wiping me off before crawling on top of me. This is where we have been for the last two hours. When I left Cash's house, I went straight to Mike's house, and picked up Liz, while Tim and Kara followed behind in their car to the only Mexican place in town. We ended up staying there for a few hours, talking about everything from Tim's talk with the detective and Kara's pregnancy, to our engagement.

"It was good. It will be nice having Kara around. I'm excited to get to know her better, and have my nephew close when he comes; plus, it will be nice having someone to help out in the shop since mom is planning on spending more time in Alabama with George."

"Yeah, and having her around will give you some time to start planning our wedding."

"Do you want a big wedding?" she asks, setting her chin on the top of her hands.

"I don't care if it's big or small, as long as when it's over, you have my last name." She smiles, lifting a finger and watching as it travels over my lips.

"I still can't believe that we're getting married," she says softly, still looking at her finger on my mouth.

"Why?"

"It's just all happening so fast," she shrugs, her eyes meeting mine.

"Not fast enough, if you ask me," I grumble.

She laughs, rolling off me to her back, covering her face with her hands. "Who knew that Trevor Earl Mayson would complain about not being tied down fast enough?"

"Tied down? I like the sound of that." I roll on top of her, pinning her hands next to her head.

"You're not tying me down," she says, her chest rising and falling quickly.

"Why not? Don't you trust me?"

"Yes."

"Let's see how much you trust me." I pull her hands up above her head, stretching her out underneath me. "Keep your hands up here." I sit up, straddling her, running my hands down over the smooth skin of her arms. I trail my fingers lower down, grazing the sides of her breasts, along her ribs. Then I use my hands to move back up her waist, cupping her breasts, trapping her nipples between my middle and pointer fingers. I

276

pull up, her body arching off the bed. "Don't move your hands." I tell her, when she goes to lift them off the bed.

"I thought you were going to tie me down?" she moans. I smile, biting the inside of my cheek to keep from laughing.

"We're working on trust. I trust you to keep your hands above your head."

"Oh." She lets out a disappointed breath, making me smile and her eyes narrow. My fiancée doesn't like to admit it, but she is definitely a dirty girl.

"Keep your hands where they are." I lean over the side of the bed, grabbing the first thing I find, which happens to be her lace panties.

"What are you doing with those?"

"You'll see," I say, pulling her up a little higher on the bed so her hands reach the headboard. I cross her wrists over one another, and then use the lacy panties. I wind them around her wrists, and then the slat in the headboard. "Now, where was I?" I look her over, before lifting both her legs with my hands and sit her ass against my thighs, wrapping her legs around my hips. "Now, let's start over." I run my palms from her stomach to her breasts, palming both, before tugging on her nipples. I watch as she arches her back, her pussy rubbing against my cock, her breasts rising and falling rapidly. I let go of her nipples, holding onto her at her ribcage. I keep one there, moving the other hand past her lower belly, then using my thumb to slide over her clit, her hips circle, rubbing against my cock again. "Hold on to the headboard, baby," I tell her, before I pull her feet from around my waist, setting them onto the bed next to my hips. I lift her slightly, flexing my hips, and slide deep inside her. Her body is completely in the air, almost like she's doing a back bend, making it easy for me to pound into her with a slight raise of my hips.

"Oh God! I'm going to pass out," she moans.

"You won't," I tell her, slamming up into her harder, one hand tugging her nipples, the other traveling lower to play with her clit.

"I'm...I'm going to pass out," she yells, as her body starts to convulse, her pussy strangling my cock.

"Fuck!" I yell, holding her hips. One, two, and three more stokes and I sit back on my calves, wrapping her legs back around my hips, then lean forward, untying her hands, pulling her up to me. Her body is boneless; her heart is beating a hundred miles an hour and both our bodies are covered in sweat.

"That was...that was...wow," she whispers, then starts to laugh. "Were you in the circus?" she laughs louder, making me laugh.

"What?" I ask, confused.

"Well, I felt like some kind of circus performer standing on my head."

"What kind of circuses have you gone to, perv?" I chuckle, making her laugh harder. Knowing that this is what I have to look forward to made me feel like a fucking king. Having a woman who was not only beautiful, but someone I could talk to about anything and laugh with was priceless.

Chapter 10

Liz

I look up as I see the door to the shop open. November walks in carrying July. "Hey, how's it going?" I ask, putting out our new shipment of handbags.

"Good! I just got back from my dad's. He had to get his July fix," November says, walking back behind the cash register to sit on the stool.

"Is he still telling you that you can move home?" I ask, laughing. Mike doesn't like to give up his time with his granddaughter, so lately, he has been telling November that she should move home so he can have full time access to her.

"No, he stopped saying that after Asher heard him and thought he was serious," she smiles. "You should have seen the look on his face."

"No way," I shake my head. "Asher happy is slightly scary. Asher mad? No thanks."

"Oh, he's not that bad," she says, kissing July all over her cute chubby face.

"So says the girl who's married to him," I laugh. The chime above the door goes off again. This time, Jen's friend Britney walks in, with Cash's baby-momma Jules. November and I share a look; both of us have been lectured about being nice. I don't know Jules at all, but if she's hanging out with Jen or Jen's friends, I'm not sure that I want to know her. "Hi, can I help you guys?" I ask them, stepping towards the front of the store.

"Do you have baby stuff?" Jules asks, rubbing her stomach.

"We have a few things, but not many. They're in that section," I say, pointing towards the back of the store.

"Thanks," Britney says. Jules walks off, leaving Britney standing in front of me, twirling her hair.

"Do you need something else?"

"You know she's pregnant with Cash's baby, so does she get, like, a discount or something?"

Britney asks, making me want to punch her in her boob.

"Nope, sorry we don't have any discounts here," I tell her, walking to where November is sitting, trying to kill Britney with her eyes.

"Oh, well, okay then," she shrugs, walking off. I do everything in my power not to roll my eyes at how big of a cliché she is, with her big boobs popping out of her top, and her even bigger bleached-out blonde hair that's in desperate need of a deep conditioner.

November shakes her head looking over at Jules, who is holding up a pair of tiny blue socks. "So, how's the wedding planning coming along?" she asks, and it's my turn to shake my head.

"Between Trevor's mom and mine, I haven't done anything. The other day, they told me that my wedding colors were going to be lavender, mint green, and silver; they also informed me that we would be getting married under the weeping willow where Trevor proposed." November laughs, making baby July smile at her. "You think that's funny?" I ask, tickling her side. She squirms, holding out her arms for me to take her. "How is it that you get cuter every day?" I ask her, kissing her cheek. Her outfit today is a hot pink top, a frilly multi-colored skirt, tights, and white socks that look like ballet flats. She gurgles, shoving her face into my neck, rubbing back and forth the way babies do when they're sleepy.

"It's almost time for a nap," November says, smiling and watching us. It's times like this, when I'm holding July, that I can forget for a second that the thought of having a child makes me panic. "So how's it working out with Kara?"

"It's been awesome having her around. I really like her."

"You guys should come to the house and visit."

"Sure, let me know when," I say. I look down, noticing that July has gone still; her eyes are closed, and her chubby little cheek is pressed into my shoulder, making her tiny mouth form a small pout. "That didn't take long." I smile, carefully handing her back over to November.

"She likes her Aunty Liz," she says, putting July over her shoulder and covering her with a thin blanket. "So, what are your plans for the night?"

"I'm not sure. I know Trevor is working; I was thinking of going out to dinner with Kara. I feel bad that she's all alone."

"Well, Asher should be home kind of early. What do you say we all meet at the Italian place on Main around six?"

"Sounds good to me."

"Alright. Well, see you then," she says, standing up and grabbing her bag. I walk her to the door, holding it open for her.

"See you at six," I say, closing the door behind her.

"I can't wait to see what Cash's baby looks like," Jules says, walking to the front of the store. I forgot that she and Britney were still here.

"Well, if he's a Mayson, I'm sure he will be cute," I say, not even thinking that my words could be misinterpreted.

"I'm carrying Cash's baby," Jules growls, leaning forward.

'I didn't mean it like that." I say softly, feeling bad.

"Whatever. Let's go, Brit," Jules says, dropping the few items she had in her hand to the floor, before walking out the door.

"Shit." I sigh, pick up the stuff she dropped, and walk to the front of the store. My phone beeps a few minutes later. When I look at it, it's a text from Trevor.

> **Trevor:** Jules called Cash bitching him out about you saying the kid wasn't his.

> **Me:** It wasn't even like that.

I text back, shaking my head at the stupidity of the whole situation.

> **Trevor:** Why would you say something like that to her?

> **Me:** I'm not even going to justify that stupid question with a response.

I type so fast that my fingers hurt.

Tossing my phone down on the counter, I walk to the back of the store to take stock.

"Anyone here?" I hear a deep male voice call from the front of the store.

"Be out in a second," I yell, breaking down the last box, before putting it in the pile with the rest. "Hi, can I help you?" I look up when I walk into the main part of the store; the man in front of me takes me off guard he's so stunning. I don't even know if a guy should be called stunning, but he is. His skin is the color of dark caramel; you can tell that his heritage is most likely Hawaiian. His long black hair is pulled back into a ponytail at the base of his neck, showing off the features of his sculptured face. His high cheekbones, square jaw, dark lashes and amber eyes would take any woman's breath away.

"Liz Hayes?" His deep voice rumbles; he's dressed in a dark grey suit, with a silk, wine-colored shirt that's unbuttoned at the neck.

"Yes," I say, swallowing hard. His energy is so scary, that I dig my fingernails into my palms to avoid running.

"I'm Kai." He sticks out his hand. I look down at it, noticing how giant it is, and quickly put my hand out. His engulfs mine.

I clear my throat, taking my hand back. "Nice to meet you, Kai," I say, his mouth twitches, then he schools his features.

"I'm looking for your brother. Do you know how I can get ahold of him?" I shake my head no.

"You're either very loyal, or very stupid." He shakes his head. "Do you understand that when the truth comes out about your brother, there will be no help for him? He's as good as dead."

"The police—"

"Won't be able to do anything for him." He interrupts sternly. He walks around the store, his hands clasped behind him; his posture is relaxed, but his energy is still beating against me, making me feel immobile. When he makes it back to me, his hand goes to the inside of his suit jacket, making me flinch. "You watch too much television, Ms. Hayes." He laughs, making me glare. "I want you to give your brother my number. I have a proposition for him."

I take the card from him, holding it tightly in my hand. "Okay," I say, as he walks to the door, opening it. Before it closes behind him, he turns his eyes on mine.

"You need to have another employee with you in the store if you're going to be in the back, Ms. Hayes," he says, sounding just like Trevor, making me roll my eyes. When I know he's gone, I run to the door and lock it.

I pick up my phone to call Tim, who answers on the third ring.

"Is Kara okay?"

"Kara is fine, but a guy stopped by my store wanting to get in touch with you."

"Are you okay?" he asks, sounding nervous.

"I'm fine, Tim, I just...I think that you should call him."

"Liz-"

He starts to say something but I cut him off I don't know why but I think that Kai might have a way of protecting Tim. "His name was Kai and he said that when the truth comes out about what you're doing not even the police will be able to protect you. He said he has a proposition for you."

I hear his sharp inhale "What's his number?" I ramble off the numbers to him listening to him scratching them down. "I'll call him sis, just promise me that you will look out for Kara."

"I promise, just be careful Tim. I know I don't really know what's going on but you have people here that love you and need you to be safe."

"Don't worry about me just take care of yourself and Kara," he says, hanging up, leaving me looking at the phone in my hand, hoping that whoever Kai is that he can help Tim out. As soon as I'm off the phone with Tim, it beeps with a message.

Trevor: Don't ever do that again.

The message leaves me speechless, and my gut clenches in anger. Part of me wants to text him back a big F-U; instead, I turn my phone off, do a last walk through of the store, and head to Mike's to pick up Kara so that we can head out to meet November for dinner.

"Where the fuck is your phone?" I hear growled from behind me. I look around the table at Kara's pale face, November's smirk, and Asher's smile. Kara and I got to the restaurant early and got a table. November and Asher showed up fifteen minutes later with a sleeping July. We all ordered dinner, and I ordered wine. After the day I had, I need something to help calm my nerves. I didn't want to tell Kara about my visitor; she was already stressed enough without dealing with anything else. When Asher first arrived, he looked at me from across the table like he was disappointed in me. That's when I lost it and told them about what happened with Jules. I told them what I had said *exactly,* and that I didn't like that the people I have come to care for thought that I was a bitch, when my words were taken wrongly, and I had apologized for being misunderstood.

I turn my head and look over my shoulder at Trevor, who is standing behind me with his arms crossed. He has another thing coming if he thinks that I'm going to be intimidated by him. "Oh, hey, honey. How are you?" I ask, turning my body to the side in my chair.

"How am I?"

"Yeah, you know, the normal greeting when you see someone that you haven't seen for any length of time."

"I see. Well, let me tell you how I am," he says, taking a step towards me, holding his fingers out in front of him. "First, I was stuck in Nashville with a flat tire. I tried to call my doting fiancée to let her know what was going on, and not to worry about me." I feel slightly bad about him being stuck but not that bad after what he messaged me so I shrug motioning my hands for him to continue on his tirade. "Second." He growls leaning forward. "I get a call from my fiancée's brother telling me about some new shit that my doting fiancée didn't even bother to call and tell me about; and again, when I tried to call and make sure she was okay, I got sent to voicemail." He takes another step towards me, his body inches from mine; he leans down, getting in my space.

"Last, but not least, I go home and find that my sweet fiancée isn't there, and hasn't left a note, making me worry and wonder if she's safe. Then, my brother calls to ask me if I'm going to be having dinner with him and my beautiful, frustrating, infuriating fiancée," he growls, his eyes narrowing.

"Well, if my handsome jerk of a fiancée would have acted like he knew me at all, and would not have accused me of doing something I didn't do, then had the nerve to tell me to never do it again, maybe I wouldn't have turned my phone off," I growl right back at him.

His jaw clenches, his eyes looking around the table before coming back to mine. "I've been worried about you." He says softly, making my anger dwindle.

"I...I want to be so mad right now," I say, wondering what the hell is wrong with me that I can't even be pissed at him for any length of time.

"You want to, but you're not." He smirks, making me want to kick him.

"Don't push your luck, Earl."

He pulls me up out of my seat, wrapping his arms around me, his face going into my neck where he whispers, "You're getting spanked for that." I bite my lip to keep from moaning; his head comes up, his eyes looking over my face. "I love you, but don't make me worry about you when it's not necessary. Even if you're pissed and you just answer your phone to tell me to fuck off, that's better than not hearing anything from you and wondering if you're okay."

"Fine." I roll my eyes, pushing at his chest, not ready to be over my snit.

"Are you done eating?"

"Yeah, we just finished."

"You dropping Kara home?"

"Yeah, I drove her here."

"Alright, I'll meet you at the house."

"Fine," I grumble, he kisses my forehead, then tilts my face back to kiss my lips. Then, he lets me go, walking around the table, patting Asher's back, kissing November's cheek, and giving Kara a hug.

"See you at home, baby," he says, before walking out the door of the restaurant.

"So, he's a quick learner," Asher says, smiling. November elbows him in the ribs, rolling her eyes, making me laugh.

"We should get home," November says, standing. Looking at Kara, she asks, "You want us to give you a ride? You're on our way."

"Sure," she shrugs, looking at me.

"That's fine. I'll just see you tomorrow at the store."

We all pull out of the restaurant at the same time, with me heading in the opposite direction of them. When I pull into the driveway, Trevor is just opening his truck door. I watch him climb down with a case of beer in his hand. He sets it on the tail of his truck and walks to my car, where he opens my door, leans in, and unbuckles me.

"You got here quick," he says, pulling me up into his arms, slamming my car door.

"Kara rode with Asher and November."

"Good," he says against my mouth, before biting my bottom lip. His hand tugs my hair to the side, his mouth opening over the skin of my neck. I love when he takes control of me. I moan, and his teeth scrape against me, traveling up to my ear and biting down. He picks me up, and then stops at his truck, grabbing the beer. I'm trying to get his clothes off as he's walking. I have his plaid shirt unbuttoned, so I bend forward, licking his chest.

"Jesus," he says, as I rub myself against him as he's trying to get the door unlocked. When the door opens, there is a loud thud, and then both his hands are on my ass. His mouth crashes into mine; one of my hands goes to his hair, the other to his belt. His mouth leaves mine, traveling down my chin and neck, then pauses at my chest, where he bites my nipple through my shirt and bra, making me moan. My hands leave him, going to my shirt, pulling it up and over my head, then to the front of my bra to unsnap it. He pins me to the wall, holding me up with his hips, before he grabs both my breasts, licking one nipple then the other. His mouth comes back to mine, his hands going to my ass and thighs, his fingers digging into my denim-covered skin as he walks us towards the bedroom.

"I need you," I say, biting his earlobe, then licking his neck. He runs us into the wall, his mouth crashing back into mine. We're both breathing heavily when he starts to undo my jeans.

"You're only allowed to wear dresses from now on," he grumbles, making me smile right before he bites my neck, then lowers his head to lick over my nipple again, making my head thud against the wall. I finally get his shirt off and drop it to the floor as I bite down onto his collarbone. He starts moving again, my nails digging into his back as he rubs his fingers along the seam of my jeans. I can feel the wetness pooling between my thighs. "I need to taste you. I've been thinking about it all day," he says, making my body shiver and become even wetter.

"Please," I whimper; just thinking about him doing that makes me crazy. I bite down on his neck, grinding against him. All of sudden, all movement stops. I think I might have bitten him too hard until I feel him start to tremble.

"What the fuck?" he yells, holding me tighter against him. I lift my head looking in his eyes, seeing that he's actually trembling in fury, and look over my shoulder to see Jen tied to our bed.

"Holy shit," I whisper, looking at Jen, who is tied spread-eagle to the bed, wearing nothing but a pair of small lace panties.

"What the fuck are you doing here?" Trevor growls, walking us to the dresser, still holding on to me tightly, my chest pressed against his. He pulls out a shirt from his drawer before he turns around, putting me on my feet, pulling the shirt over my head. "Are you okay?" His hands come to my face, pulling my eyes to his. When I see the worried look on his face, I take a step back. My stomach drops when he reaches out for me desperately, but I take another step back, then another, until I reach the bedroom door, motioning for him to step out. He looks at the bed, then me; my blood that was simmering before, starts to boil. I was going to kill this crazy bitch. I look in her direction to see her watching us, not saying anything. I don't want to look at her again until Trevor is out of the room. He walks towards me, his head low. He tries to touch me, but I shake my head; my whole body is buzzing with anger. When he finally steps out the door, I close and lock it behind him. I turn around to see Jen watching me; her mouth is moving, but she's not saying anything. I walk towards her. Her eyes following me, getting wider the closer I get.

"So you thought that you would come here, tie yourself up, and when Trevor got home, he would see you in bed and screw your brains out?" I ask, looking at the knots on her ankles, realizing that someone else must have tied her up, because her hands are tied the same way, and just as tight.

"What are you doing here?" she whispers, looking at the door. I think she's in shock or something; this girl never stops running her mouth and now she can't even form a few words.

"Don't act like you don't know that I live here."

"You weren't supposed to be here." The anger in her voice makes my eyebrows go up.

"I wasn't supposed to come home to my own house?"

"He doesn't even want you!" she yells, her body thrashing around on the bed.

"You do know that we're getting married, right?" I cross my arms over my chest, looking down at her.

"He *will* come back to me."

"Wow," "You are completely insane!"

"How do you think I got tied up?" She stops moving and smirks; I can't help but to laugh at how stupid she is. Then I think about it; if I would have dropped Kara home and come in later, her plan might have worked. And that thought pisses me off even more.

"For someone who has so many stalker tendencies, you don't know much," I say, looking around the room, noticing her bag on the dresser.

"I'm not a st–stalker," she sputters out, looking around, pulling on her wrist and trying to get free.

"Really, are you sure? Because I'm almost positive that this is the kind of thing a stalker does." I open her purse, find her phone, and go to her text messages. Finding exactly what I'm looking for, I press call.

"What are you doing with my phone?" she yells. I take the blanket from the end of the bed and toss it over her, with a self-reminder to burn all the bedding when she leaves.

"Hi, Mr. Carlson. Jen is here at Trevor's and is going to need you to come pick her up. Oh, and if she comes back again, I will be pressing charges for breaking and entering."

"You fucking bitch! What the fuck is wrong with you? Are you crazy?" she screams, thrashing harder than before. I knew she wouldn't like that; she's a daddy's girl all the way. Plus, her daddy pays for her school, and whatever else she needs, so his anger affects her bank account.

"I'm going to say this one last time, Jen. Trevor is mine, and if you insist on doing things like this, I will insist on making your life a living hell."

"I'm going to tell everyone in town to stop coming to your store so that you're forced out of business!" she yells.

"You can do that, and I'm sure some of your minions will listen; but that won't change the fact that Trevor is mine."

"He will be back. They all come back, eventually," she says, making my anger skyrocket. I look around, seeing the scissors that I used this morning to cut a tag off a shirt laying on the dresser.

"What do you think about girls with bangs?" I ask, looking her over.

"What?"

"You know, bangs," I say, making a slashing motion with my finger across my forehead.

"No one wears bangs," she says, rolling her eyes.

"You have always been a trendsetter, right, Jen?"

"Are you out of your mind? You want to talk about hair and clothes? Fucking untie me!" she screeches. I pick the scissors up off the table, and walk to the bed. Jen's eyes go wide, looking at me then the scissors in my hand. "Look, I'm sorry, okay? Please don't kill me." I can't help the evil smile that slides into place; her eyes get huge, and

I lift the scissors close to her, speaking very quietly.

"You're going to want to be very still, Jen. You don't want me to give you crooked bangs or to cut you, right?" I ask, gathering a large chunk of hair from the front of her head.

"Don't you dare," she growls, but doesn't move.

"Be still," I repeat in a sugary sweet voice, before I open the scissors over the large wad of hair, and begin to cut; the noise that the scissors make is music to my ears. When I'm done, she has bangs that are so short, that ninety percent of her forehead shows. "Wow, I never noticed how big your forehead is. Too bad you don't like bangs; they could help to cover that shit up," I tell her, shaking my head. "I'm sure your dad will be here soon; I better go," I say, dropping her hair in the trashcan by the bed, taking the scissors with me.

"I'm going to fucking kill you."

I shrug and walk out of the room closing the door behind me. Trevor is standing against the wall his head back, looking at the ceiling. Jen starts yelling from the other side of the door to untie her, so I yell back that her dad can do it when he gets here, causing her to start screaming at the top of her lungs. I have one last wicked idea.

I walk over to my purse where I had dropped it by the door when Trevor had carried me inside. I grab my phone, walk back into the bedroom, snap a few pictures of Jen, and grin when she thrashes around on the bed so hard, I think her wrists might snap. "There," I say. "You're always taking selfies when I see you and your posse in my store and at the bar. These will be a nice addition to your collection you no doubt have on Facebook. Don't worry; I'll tag ya."

"Oh my God! Don't you dare, Liz!" she hisses.

"Then if I were you, I would think twice about what you do after your dad comes to get you," I taunt. That shuts her up.

When I walk back out of the bedroom, Trevor's eyes come to mine. "I'm sorry, baby," he whispers, pulling me into him. My arms go around his waist; we stay like that for a little while, just holding each other, then I look around, realizing that Lolly is missing.

"Where's Lolly?' I ask, running down the hall, yelling for her. She's not anywhere in the house. I run back to our room, throwing the door open, causing it to slam into the wall. "Where is my dog?" I yell, moving towards the bed, ready to kill this bitch. She must see how serious I am because she answers right away.

"Th...the shed out back." It takes everything in me not to smack her in the face, or suffocate her with a pillow.

"I got her, baby," Trevor yells from the living room. I run and skid to a halt, seeing Lolly stumbling around.

"What's wrong with her?" I get down on my knees; when she sees me, she stumbles in my direction, and then flops down in front of me. Laying my ear against her chest, I listen to her heart and make sure that she is breathing okay.

"Bitch, I'm calling the fucking cops!" I hear Trevor yell, and then Jen apologizing over and over again.

I can't believe she did this! She broke in, drugged our dog, and then put her in the shed so that her friend could tie her to our bed. Trevor comes back into the living room with the phone to his ear, his eyes on me. He looks like he could kill someone. "Dad, I need you to come to my house, and bring someone with you. Jen broke in, drugged Lolly, and is tied to my bed." His hand goes to his hair. With his chest heaving every time he looks at me, he seems to get angrier. "Fuck no! She did this shit herself, thinking that I would want her fucking ass," he roars into his phone, making Lolly jump. He pulls the phone away from his ear, shoving it in his back pocket. I stand and walk towards him, wrapping myself around him. I hate that he's feeling like this.

"Are you okay?"

"Fuck no," he says, holding me tighter.

"Well, this has got to be the most interesting day that I have ever had," I say, right before the doorbell starts going off. "That's probably her dad." I unwind myself from Trevor, but he stops me from going to the door with a hand in the back of my shirt.

"I'll get it. You stay with Lolly."

"Sure."

He bends, kissing my forehead, then heads to the front door, while I go back to Lolly, who is still laying down next to one of the chairs in the living room. "You'll be okay, girl." When Trevor walks back into the living room, Jen's dad is close behind him; his face is bright red, and he looks ready for murder.

"Ms. Hayes, I am very sorry that this happened. Please accept my deepest apologies, and know that something like this will never happen again."

"All due respect, John, I'm pressing charges against Jen for what she did. Not only did she break into my house, but she drugged my dog, then had someone tie her to my and my fiancée's bed," Trevor says, his fists clenched at his sides.

"I understand," Jen's dad says, before turning at the sound of someone walking into the house.

"John."

"James." The two men greet each other.

"Where is she? I would like to speak with her," Jen's dad says. It's plain to see that he's holding absolute fury in check.

"She's down the hall, the last door on the right. She only has a blanket covering her, sir," I tell him. He looks taken aback, and then shakes his head, walking down the hall to his daughter.

"You all right, son?" James asks, looking at Trevor, whose jaw is so tight that I'm surprised it doesn't break.

"Yeah, but I still want to press charges."

"Alright, why don't you and I go outside and talk for a few minutes, and you can tell me what exactly happened."

"Sure. Just give me a minute with Liz and I'll meet you out there."

James nods before he comes to me, squatting down. "Hey, darlin'. You alright?" He asks softly, and I nod, thinking that I'm a big fat liar. "Sure you are." He smiles, pulling me forward to kiss my forehead, then stands, walking out the door.

"You okay, baby?" Trevor asks, squatting the same way his dad had.

"Yeah, I'm just ready for this day to be over with," I say, laying my head against Lolly's side. Trevor's hand runs over my cheek and back through my hair.

"Everyone will be gone soon."

"Alright," I whisper, trying not to think about what would have happened if I had walked in while Trevor was here alone with Jen. I would like to say that I am so secure in our relationship that I wouldn't have assumed the worst; but the truth is, I, like a lot of women, would have jumped to conclusions, never thinking that this was some kind of sick setup.

"I'm going to be right outside talking to Dad." He bends, kissing my cheek.

Ten minutes later, Trevor and his dad come back inside. Lolly is finally up and about, but still stumbling into things when she tries to walk.

"Are they still in the room?" James asks, looking down the hall.

"Yeah." Just then, Jen comes down the hall, tears streaming down her face, her new bangs showing off her large forehead that she tries to cover with her hand. I bite my lip to keep from laughing at how bad she looks. Trevor, who is standing next to his dad, looks up when he hears her; his eyes go wide, then come to me. The look on his face makes me pull Lolly close and shove my face into her fur to muffle the sound of my laughter.

"Sheriff," Jen's dad says. I raise my head slightly so that I can see their interaction.

"Mr. Carlson, why don't we talk outside?" James says, holding his hand out in front of him for Jen and her father to precede him. Jen hasn't looked up; her dad places his hand against her lower back, leading her out of the house. When I hear the sound of the door closing, I can feel Trevor staring at me. I don't look up; I just sit there and continue to pet Lolly.

"I didn't know you wanted to be a hair dresser."

"I didn't." I finally look up to see Trevor watching me closely. "Um...I may have gotten a wee bit angry."

"Well, remind me when I piss you off to never leave any sharp objects laying around."

"Don't piss me off." I shrug. He takes a step towards me, where I'm sitting on the floor, bending low so his mouth is next to my ear.

"You love my dick, baby. Maybe even more than I do. And don't think I've forgotten about the stunt you pulled today."

"I already told you; I never said anything to Jules," I growl, pissed off.

"I know you didn't, and I was wrong to jump to conclusions. But you still turned off your phone, making it so I couldn't get in touch with you; then you didn't tell me about the visitor you had at the store."

"Oh."

"Oh." He smirks. "What do you think your punishment should be?"

"You're not punishing me." My eyes narrow; his eyes drop to my mouth. He leans in, giving me a quick kiss.

"We'll see," he shrugs, standing back up.

"I'm serious, Trevor; you're not punishing me," I say, beginning to panic.

"When you get it, you won't be thinking of it as a punishment."

"What the hell does that mean?"

"You guys okay?" James asks, walking in. My face turns bright red, wondering how much he might have heard.

"We're good, Dad. Just making plans," Trevor says, looking down and winking at me. My mouth drops open. I have never seen him wink, and he has a good one, unlike mine. Once, when I tried to wink at someone, they thought I had something in my eye and offered me Visine. If that's not an ego-crusher, I don't know what is.

"Mr. Carlson and Jen just left," James says, walking into the kitchen, pulling out a note pad. Trevor holds out his hand, helping me up off the floor. He pulls me flush against him.

"I love you, baby."

"Always?" I ask, standing on my tiptoes.

"Always." Kissing my lips, then my forehead, he turns me around, scooting me towards the kitchen.

"So, you're going to need to sign a few things and decide if you want to apply for a restraining order."

"Do you think that will be necessary?" I ask, worrying my bottom lip.

"I never thought you would need to press charges against Jen Carlson; so the question you need to ask yourself is: can you trust Jen to leave you alone?"

"I don't know," I say quietly. This is just one more thing that I did not want to deal with right now. Trevor rubs circles along my back, his touch helping to calm me. "What do you think?" I ask, looking over my shoulder at Trevor.

"I want you safe. I know that a piece of paper is not going to stop her if she tries to do something stupid; but if we do this, she may back off."

"She didn't attack me. She was here trying to get you back; she just went about it in a really stupid way. How did she even get inside?" I ask.

"She claims to have a key." James says looking at Trevor.

"You gave her a key?" I ask looking at Trevor as well.

"Fuck no." He growls his jaw ticking. "And I don't know how she got in. All I know is she broke into our home and drugged our dog. I would say that both those things point to her being unstable wouldn't you?"

"Yes." I sigh, ready for this day to be over.

"So it's settled; we're getting a restraining order, and if we don't need it, good."

"I think that would be the smart thing to do," James says, looking between Trevor and me. "So, Susan says the wedding is planned for two weeks from now."

"What?" I'm shocked. I have no idea what he's talking about.

"Mom called today, baby. Well, actually, it was a conference call between both of our moms. They tried to get ahold of you, with no luck, so they called me. The pastor that married your mom and dad is only available that weekend; after that, he flies back to Nicaragua, where he's helping to build a community center and won't be available for a few more months. So I told them to go ahead and book him."

"You told them to go ahead? You do know that I haven't even gotten my dress, right? Our moms have completely trampled me."

"You can find a dress. I don't care if you show up in jeans; I am not waiting any longer for you to be my wife."

"Why do we need to rush this? We already live together."

"We're living in sin."

"We're living in sin?" I repeat, shaking my head. Then I look over at James, and when I see his giant smile, I want to scream.

"You better find your dress, baby, because even if I have to carry you down the aisle over my shoulder in two weeks, you are going to be Elizabeth Star Mayson."

"This is crazy, you're crazy, and our moms are crazy," I ramble. "I have no idea what I'm going to do."

"Calm down; it's going to be okay." I look up at Trevor, who now looks worried. Good. He should be worried. "They said everything was taken care of; all you have to do was show up."

"Do you know that little girls start planning their weddings from the time they're young and get their first Barbie doll? They dream of what it's going to look like, the colors they will choose, the style of their dress…" I trail off, shaking my head.

"You did that?" He asks incredulously, looking down at me with wonder.

"No." I shake my head at him. "But if I had, it wouldn't matter, because they have taken over everything. I thought, *At least I get to pick out my dress*, but it sounds like they have taken over that as well." I watch as Trevor and his dad start laughing. "What the hell is so funny?" I yell, as the guys laugh. Lolly comes into the kitchen; she's no longer stumbling around. I breathe a sigh of relief that she's going to be okay.

"Nothing, baby. If you want to pick your dress, you pick your dress."

"They already did," I pout, making Trevor shake his head and look at his dad.

"I will tell them that you're getting your own dress."

"Fine," I harrumph, and cross my arms over my chest like a bratty five-year-old.

"But you need to have it in two weeks. I don't know how much time it takes to pick a dress, but you better get started."

"Fine," I say, and Trevor smiles at his dad.

"Do you need anything else, Dad?" he asks, then looks back down at me and suddenly, I don't want James to leave.

"No, son. I go—"

"No! Don't you need me to, like, tell you what happened?" I cut him off.

"Trevor already told me, honey."

"But he told you what *he* saw. What about what *I* saw?"

"Like Jen's bangs?" James asks, smirking.

"Ugh...I...um...well, you know. Oh, look at the time! It's getting late. You should go," I say, standing quickly. I can hear Trevor chuckle, so I elbow him in the ribs while smiling at James.

"Yeah, I need to drop these papers off at the station before I head home." He pulls me in for a hug. "Love ya', honey," he says, bringing tears to my eyes.

"Love you, too," I say, wiping my eyes, taking a step back into Trevor, who wraps his arms around me. He rests his chin on the top of my head.

"You're gonna need to come down to the station tomorrow to fill out the papers for the restraining order."

"We'll be there," Trevor says, walking us forward, following his dad to the front door. "Later, Dad," he says, shutting the door behind him.

"Are you okay?"

"Yeah."

"You tired?"

"No, not really."

"Good. Then it's time for your punishment."

"No!" I squeal, trying to get free.

"Oh yeah," he says, spinning me around, pressing me into the wall. His mouth crashes into mine, his hand going to my breast, and his fingers pinching my nipple through the material of his tee shirt that I'm wearing. He takes my hands in his, pulling them up over my head. "Keep them there."

"But I—"

"No. Move them, and I stop." He bites my lip, pulling it through his teeth; his hands at the bottom of the tee lift it slowly up my waist, and then over my breasts, and finally over my head and arms. Once I'm shirtless, his fingers begin working on the button of my jeans. Once free, he tugs them over my hips, but doesn't pull them all the way off, keeping my thighs bound together by my jeans. "Remember, don't move your hands," he says against my ear, his breath causing goose bumps to break out over my skin.

His body leaves me, his hands going to the buttons of his shirt. Once he's done, he pulls it off, tossing it onto the floor. His thumb travels over my bottom lip, down my chin, his hand opening over my neck, his other hand following the same path until my breasts are in his hands. "You're beautiful, baby; but your tits are fucking amazing." He leans forward, licking over one nipple, then the other. My stomach is in knots. I can feel myself clench, my clit throbbing, begging for attention. I love when he's like this; it's hotter than any book I've ever read.

His mouth comes back to mine, his body pressing me hard against the wall, his hands on my face controlling my every move. One hand travels down along the side of my neck, along the side of my breast, my ribs, and my hip, playing along the edge of my panties, fingers tracing the lacy edge below my belly button.

"Please touch me," I beg, wanting to feel his fingers on me, and in me.

"I will," he says, but doesn't move his hand from the edge of my panties. His other hand knots in the back of my hair, pulling my head back and deepening the kiss. I feel his fingers slowly lower, until one lightly runs over my clit, making my hips jump forward towards his hand. His finger continues to graze over my clit, while his mouth works over mine, licking and biting. When he presses two fingers inside me, I moan into his mouth, my hips bucking, trying to urge him on. He pulls away, sliding slowly over my clit again.

"Stop teasing me." I was so close.

"You want to come?"

"Yes," I hiss when his fingers move quicker. I can feel the hard length of him press into my side; my hands above my head itch to touch him. Finally, I go off; the moan that escapes my mouth into his sounds wild. I can feel myself trying to pull his fingers deeper. When he pulls his hand away, I sag against the wall, my body feeling limp. The aftershocks of my orgasm still thumping through my blood, I don't even notice when he pulls my pants completely off until my leg is being tossed over his shoulder and his mouth is latching onto me. I look down at him; his face buried between my legs, the sight alone causing a second orgasm. "Oh God!" My head falls back against the wall; my hands lower to his head, my hands running over his hair. Two fingers enter me quickly, and I scream his name, thrashing my head back and forth, trying to push him away. "It's too much! Please, it's too much." I try to move, but he holds me tighter, his fingers moving faster inside of me.

When he sucks on my clit, I swear that I'm going to pass out. He drops my leg, and he presses his body tightly to mine, holding me up. I can hear his zipper, then I'm lifted; my legs circle his hips, and he pulls me down, impaling me on him. "Fuck," he growls, lifting and lowering me onto him. I pull his mouth to mine, biting first his top, then his bottom lip, before my tongue seeks his.

His hips start thrusting faster. "You're so perfect." My face goes into his neck, my body wrapping completely around him. There is not one part of us that isn't touching. I suck on his neck, and when I feel my orgasm begin to build again, he presses me deeper into the wall; his hand comes between our sweat-soaked bodies, his thumb pressing into my clit. "You need to come with me."

"I know," I breathe, lifting my head and watching his face. His eyes are dark, his skin glistening with sweat. We stare at each other, his thumb moving in faster circles. I can feel myself begin to tighten around him. He slows down, letting me feel every inch of him slide in and out of me; the head of his cock dragging against my g-spot, causing my orgasm to slam into me without warning. His hand goes back to my ass as he starts rocking hard and fast, lifting and dropping me onto him. I can feel him expand inside me, his hands squeezing me so hard I know I will have his fingerprints on my skin when this is over. His movements start to become erratic right before he plants himself inside me, roaring my name. His face goes into my neck; our breathing is labored and our bodies are covered in sweat. The coolness of the wall behind me feels amazing against my overheated skin. He turns us around, then slides down the wall, sitting on the floor.

"I don't know how I got so lucky," he says into my neck, causing goose bumps to break out over my skin.

"I'm the lucky one." I tell him honestly. I never knew that I would find someone who loved me so completely, who made me feel beautiful, safe, and important.

"No." He lifts his head, and pulling mine from his neck, his hands hold my face gently. "I'm the lucky one. I didn't think that I would ever want someone to have the kind of power over me that you hold. I know that my future is going to be amazing because you're going to be by my side; and with you, everything is better," he says, leaning in, touching his mouth to mine. When he pulls away, I feel tears falling down my cheeks.

"Ditto," I say on a sob, shoving my face back into his neck.

"Jesus. I love you so fucking much; you would think I was growing a vagina."

"I love you more."

"Impossible," he whispers, kissing my head. "Let's get up and shower."

"You'll have to carry me."

"My pants are around my ankles. If I try carrying you right now, we're both going to end up on the floor."

"Okay. Let me see if my legs work." I untangle myself from around his hips.

"I hate that."

"What?" I ask, my eyebrows drawing together. I pick up his flannel shirt and put it on, wrapping it around me like a robe.

"Your heat, I hate losing it." He stands, pulling up his jeans; and I wrap my arms around him, shoving my face into his chest, breathing him in. "Shower," he says, swinging me up into his arms, carrying me into the bathroom. That night after we stripped the bed, Trevor in his normal position, his body on top of mine—I thank my dad for sending me a man like Trevor. I don't know why, but I know that he has something to do with Trevor being placed in my life.

Chapter 11

Trevor

"I thought we talked about this?" I look at Liz, and then back down at the round case of pills that are taunting me from the counter. I told her that I want to start working on getting her pregnant. I need to know that she is tied to me in a way that is unbreakable. Yeah, she has my ring on her finger, and in a week she'll have my last name. But that's not going to be enough. It might make me a controlling dick, but I need it. I have to know that we have something to tie us together through eternity.

"No, *you* talked about it. You said what you wanted, and I told you that I don't want the same thing."

"Baby, I know you want the same thing as me."

"In Trevor's universe, I'm sure you think that." She stands, taking her plate to the sink.

"You love July." My anger is starting to surface, and I know that I need to stop before I say something I can't take back.

"I do," she whispers. I can see tears forming in her eyes.

"Talk to me; tell me what the fuck is going through your head?" I yell. Her eyes meet mine, and there is so much pain looking back at me that I flinch.

"I can't do it," she whispers, right before she runs out of the house. It takes a second to realize that the sound I hear is her car spitting up gravel in the driveway. "Fuck!" I roar, picking up her pill case and crushing it in my fist, before I throw them across the room, grab my keys, and head out to find my fiancée.

I have driven all over town, and called everyone and anyone who might know where Liz is, but no one has heard a word from her. Logically, I know that she's okay, but I feel sick with worry and know I won't be able to breathe easy until I can see her and touch her. Something in my brain makes me drive by the cemetery where her father is buried. When I see her car parked outside the gate, all the things I didn't understand, the things she has been keeping bottled up, slide into place. Shutting off the engine, I hop out of the truck and walk through the giant iron gates. I look to the left, seeing a bright blue blur off in the distance. When I get closer, I see Liz kneeling, her head to the ground in front of her father's grave. Watching her small body shaking with sobs, my gut tightens, and my stomach drops. Seeing the woman I love in this kind of pain kills me. Once I reach her, I pull her into my arms, breathing her in.

"I can't do it. I love you, but I can't have your baby," she cries, her voice filled with so much pain that it feels like my skin is splitting open.

"Baby, what happened to your mom and dad is not going to happen to me and you." I feel her trying to climb into me; I hold her closer, trying to absorb some of her pain. "Your dad would want you to be as happy as possible," I whisper into her hair, running my hands up and down her back, trying to comfort her.

"I'm af—afraid that I'll leave a kid behind like I was left behind. I d—d—don't want that to happen," she stutters out, her body rocking against mine with the strength of her tears.

"Breathe, baby." I'm trying to speak quietly, stroking my hand down her back. "You know that we can't predict the future, but you and I not sharing the love that we have for each other with a life that we create together would be devastating to me. I love you so much more than I ever thought was possible to love another person. You have made me a better person, taught me that love—real love—is unconditional, and has no strings attached, and is given without expecting anything in return." I pull her face away from my body so I can see her eyes. "I want to share everything with you. All the good and the bad that life has to offer, I want you by my side for all of it.

"What happens if one or both of us dies? What happens then?"

"You can't live your life thinking 'what if'. There are too many variables." I tell her honestly. "Do you think that if your dad knew that he was going to leave you while he was still young, while you were still young, that he wouldn't have wanted the time he had with you, Tim, and your mom? Or do you think that even with his time cut short, that he appreciated every single second that he had with y'all, knowing that he had his family and people who loved him."

"He left me!" She cries harder.

"He did leave, but he never left you. He is always with you."

"I miss him."

"I know you do, baby," I struggle out against the lump in my throat. "I know you do."

"I don't want anyone to miss me." Her words are so quiet, that I hardly make them out.

"If something happened to you, I wouldn't know how to go on without you. I would miss you every day; so would everyone else that you have given even the smallest amount of your time to. Every person you come in contact with is lucky to know someone like you. Knowing the kind of woman you are lets me know that when you become the mother to our children, they will be lucky, because you love so completely with everything you have."

"I don't know if I can do it."

"Tell me," I say, pulling her face out of my neck, looking into her eyes. As much as it would kill me to not have a child with her, if that is what she truly wanted, I would do it for her. "You don't want a baby?" Her face goes slack; tears start to fall harder.

"When I think about never having a baby, it makes me feel sick," she whispers. "But when I think about having a baby, I feel panic." I nod my head in understanding.

"Have you ever talked to anyone about losing your dad?" She shakes her head. "Would you, if I went with you?"

"Do you think I'm crazy?"

"No, baby. I think that you haven't ever had a chance to deal with losing your dad. Maybe talking to someone will help you get some closure."

"I'm not ready to have a baby, Trevor. I love you and know that it's something that you want, but I just...I'm not ready. I don't know if I will ever be ready." As much as her words make my heart ache, I know she's right. Until she is completely ready, it wouldn't be fair to force something on her that could give her anxiety; especially when it is supposed to be something that is celebrated.

"When, or if, you're ever ready, we will talk about it then."

"I don't want to prevent you from having a family."

"You're my family, and if you're all I have for the rest of my days, I will be okay with that." She starts crying again, this time harder than before. "It will be okay, baby. One day at a time, we will work through this."

"I don't want to lose you."

"I'm not going anywhere; not without you."

"Okay."

"Okay," I say back. "Let's go home."

"Please." I walk back out of the cemetery with Liz tucked under my arm. When we reach her car, I look down at her. Her beautiful eyes are puffy and red; she looks exhausted.

"I'm gonna call the boys and have them come get your car to bring it home so you don't have to drive."

"I'm okay."

"I know, but you're not driving. Get in the truck; I'm going to move your car over to the parking lot."

"Fine," she grumbles, making me smile for the first time today.

"Be right back." I open the truck door, lifting her in, pull her face down to mine, and give her a quick kiss, before slamming the door closed. I jog to her car, slide behind the wheel, pull it into the parking lot, and shove the keys under the seat. I call Nico, asking him if he can have someone drop him off and drive Liz's car home for me. He agrees immediately; I hang up and jog back across the parking lot to where my truck is parked in front of the cemetery, open the door, and slide in. "How do you feel about taking a nap?" I ask, pulling her across the seat by the waist of her jeans.

"I could use a nap, but I'm supposed to meet the seamstress for my last fitting." As soon as the words are out, her body stiffens. I can see the wheels in her head turning.

"If you even think for one fucking minute that we're not getting married next week, you're out of your damn mind," I growl, a little more anger leaking into my words than I wanted, but fuck that; we're getting married.

"Are you sure?"

"Fuck yes." I watch as she chews her lower lip, her eyes coming to mine. "I told you before that one way or another, we're getting married. Even if I have to drag you down the damn aisle, you will have my last name in a week."

"Then I need to go have my last fitting."

"What time?" She looks at the dash, then back to me.

"Six."

"Alright, we have a few hours. We can go home and relax till then." I put the truck in drive, flipping a U-turn onto the main road. Once on the road, I pull her under my arm; her head lays against my chest, and the silence of the cab allows me to concentrate on her even breathing, the sound so soothing that my body relaxes, and I just enjoy the feel of her next to me. The entire way home, I think for the first time how easily this could be lost, and how lost I would be without it.

~~*

It's been five days since Liz broke down about having a baby. Five days of wedding planning, lots of laughter, and tons of family. Tomorrow, I marry the woman I will be spending the rest of my life with. This last week has been good for Liz—for the both of us, really. For the first time ever, Liz spoke to her mom about her father's death. Her mom surprised Liz by telling her that shortly after she and Liz started to rebuild their relationship, she started seeing a counselor to help her work through the grief she was feeling. I was pissed when Liz told me this, mad that she never thought to have her children talk to someone about their own feelings and what they were going through. I wanted to rage about the situation, but logically knew it would do no one any good to have me flip the fuck out about something that happened years ago.

After Liz talked with her mom, she agreed that it was time to talk to someone about how she's been feeling, and the fear she lives with every day, thinking that something bad is going to happen to her or someone she loves. I never knew how much she had been holding in until the day of her first session, two days after her breakdown in the cemetery. She called me, asking if I could come get her from the building where her doctor's practice was. I could hear the tears in her voice when I answered; she sounded so lost. When we got home, she opened up about the conversation she had with her doctor. She said he explained that she had a form of anxiety, and a mild case of PTSD, brought on by the loss of her father and the lack of acceptance from her mother after his death. The doctor explained that with sessions and medication, she would be able to learn how to process what she is feeling in a positive manner, instead of trying to bury it the way she always has. I know that it's going to be a lot of work for her, but I also know my woman is strong and can handle anything; and if there is ever a point when she thinks she won't be able to make it, I will pick her up and carry her.

"Baby, seriously, hurry the fuck up. We're already late!" I yell down the hall towards the bedroom.

"Hold your damn horses, Trevor!" she yells back, making me smile.

"You really going to make us late to our own rehearsal dinner?"

"If you would stop bugging me, I would be ready already," she yells back, making me laugh. I walk to the fridge, pull out a beer, pop the top, and look down at Lolly, who is watching me, waiting for the treat she knows I'm going to give her. I lean over the counter, lift the lid on the treat jar, listening to Lolly's tail as she beats a hole in the floor. "You should at least give her a command when you give her a treat, so she knows why she's getting it," Liz says. My head comes up, and my dick becomes instantly hard. My mouth falls open, and my gut clenches at the sight of her. The navy blue all-lace dress is completely form–fitting; the neck is square-cut right above her cleavage, under her collarbones. Her long blonde hair flows over her shoulders and breasts. The sleeves are long, to her wrists, and the hem reaches mid–thigh, drawing attention to her long legs.

"Do you have anything on under that?" I ask, looking her over. My eyes fall on her shoes; they are tall, with straps wrapping around her ankles, and a heel that I want to feel in my back later tonight.

"Yes, it's made to look like you don't have anything on under it."

"I don't know if I should let you out of the house looking like you do right now."

"What?"

"Every man who sees you is going to be picturing you naked under it."

"You're the only one who gets to see me naked," she smiles.

"Come here."

"I'm right here," she says, taking stuff from one bag and putting it into another, not even looking up at me.

"And I want you right here," I tell her, leaning over the counter and grabbing her hand, dragging her over to me.

"What are you doing?"

"Seeing what you've got on under this thing," I say, looking her over and seeing that the lace does have some kind of mesh under it that is the same exact tone as her skin.

"Are you happy now?" she laughs.

"Not yet; one more thing." I pull the bottom of her dress up her thighs and over her ass.

"What are you doing?"

"I want to see what I will be getting later tonight." I look at the nude-colored lace that sits under her belly button and shows off the cheeks of her ass.

"You're getting your hand, buddy." She pats my chest. "I'm staying at my mom's tonight, remember?" Fuck, I forgot about that.

"Who made that stupid rule up?"

"I don't know," she shrugs, shimmying her dress back over her hips.

"You're not leaving me tonight until I taste you; so you need to figure out how to make that happen, or your mom's going to be pissed when I show up at her house, telling her that I need to eat her daughter's pussy before I go to bed or else I can't sleep." I watch her cheeks turn bright pink as she glares at me.

"You wouldn't dare."

"Oh, but wouldn't I?" I smirk. I wouldn't do that, exactly, but I would show up at her mom's to get my nightly snack.

"Trevor."

"Figure it out, babe."

"I'm sure that you will be okay for one night," she says, the pink in her cheeks getting darker, traveling along her neck.

"It's mine. There is no reason for me to go without." We both stare at each other; her eyes darken, her breathing picks up, and I know she wants it. "Do you have everything you need?" I ask, my voice sounding a little rougher than normal. I watch as she looks around, then presses her knees together. The movement is small, but so telling.

"Yeah, but will you carry my overnight bag for me? It's still on the bed."

"No problem. Why don't you go wait in the car? I'll be there in a minute. Matter of fact..." I say, swinging her up into my arms, making her scream. "I'll just carry you out first. I don't want you walking in the gravel in those shoes." She runs her finger along my bottom lip like she always does, before relaxing into me as I carry her to the car. When we finally make it to the rehearsal dinner, we have an amazing time, surrounded by all the people who mean the most to us. We talk and share stories; both our moms put together a slideshow of each of us growing up, and even though I can see the sadness in Liz's eyes in the pictures that were taken after her father's passing, I can tell she never let it hold her back. And I promised myself that every day, I would try to make her smile. And no matter what happens she will know how much she is loved.

After the dinner, I take Liz with me out to my truck under the pretense of getting something she needs. Really, I'm getting something *I* need. I sit her on the passenger's seat of my truck, her legs hanging out the door. I lift the bottom of her dress up over her hips and eat her pussy, while she bites into her hand so people won't hear her screaming my name in the parking lot. Just when I finish with her, her mom shows up, saying it's time to go. Liz hops out of my truck, promising to see me at the wedding. I press her into the side of my truck, kissing her enough to hold me over for the night.

When I get home and finally lay down, I realize that if God is good to me, I will never have to feel her side of the bed empty again.

~~*

"Can I have your attention?" We all look up when my dad starts to talk.

After I got up this morning, all my brothers showed up. I had no idea what Liz would be doing, but I sat around playing Call of Duty, laughing, and joking with my brothers until it was time to put on our suits. We headed out to Liz's grandparents' property that was now owned by a middle-aged couple who didn't have any children. They were more than happy to let us borrow a piece of their property for the day that had meant so much to Liz and her mom.

When we arrived at the location—the part of the property that used to house a barn but had burnt to the ground years ago—that was now turned into a giant parking lot. Leading down to the location of the old weeping willow, was a path made up of small wooden posts with ribbon wrapped around them to help guide the way of our guests. There were three giant white tents set up off to the side; that would be where we had our reception later on in the evening. At the tree where we would be getting married, someone had gathered the branches of the weeping willow and tied lavender and mint-green ribbons around them, creating a space in the tree so we could stand inside and people could still see us. The old swing was painted white, the rope wrapped in gauze. The chairs for guests were set up outside of the tree, all white with lavender or mint bows tied around each one.

Even as a guy, I had to hand it to our mothers; they went above and beyond making the whole area look magical, and I knew that when Liz saw what had been done for us, she would be more than grateful, just as I was. When the time finally came for Liz to arrive, I took my place under the tree, with Cash standing beside me as my best man. The pastor that had married Liz's parents stood on my other side. I didn't know what to expect when I saw Liz on our wedding day, walking towards me. But I never expected to be floored by how beautiful she looked in her white strapless dress. The top looked like a corset, and the bottom flowed out, looking like something a southern belle would wear.

My emotions were all over the place. Pride, lust, protectiveness, possessiveness, and so much love that I thought I would explode as it coursed through me. As she walked towards me, I knew that this was exactly where I was supposed to be.

When she finally stood in front of me, I couldn't help but to put my fingers into her hair that was half–up and half–down, and pull her up to me for a kiss. I whispered to her how beautiful she was and how lucky I was to be the one she walked down the aisle to. I didn't stop whispering to her or kissing her, until I heard the pastor behind us clear his throat and say lowly that we were supposed to wait until after our vows for the kiss. I pulled back slightly, but kept my body pressed into her.

I have no idea if anyone heard our vows. I was so enraptured by her and the moment that nothing else mattered. When I slid the other part of her ring onto her finger, completing the set that would sit on her finger for the rest of our lives, I felt whole for the first time ever. And I knew she must have felt something similar when she slid my ring on my finger. Her hands were shaking, and her words low; she looked at the ring on my finger for a long time, before looking up at me with tears sliding down her cheeks that I slid away with my thumbs. The moment the pastor announced us man and wife, and that I could kiss the bride, I held her face in my hands and poured my soul into that kiss, telling her without words how happy I was.

My dad's voice snaps me out of my daydream.

"When Trevor came to me and his mother, and told us that he was going to ask Liz to marry him, we couldn't have been more proud of his choice in a wife." I look down at Liz and kiss her forehead. "It's a great honor to us as parents, seeing the boys we raised into men, choosing the kind of women our sons have chosen, and knowing that our family will grow and become bigger and better with each new addition. Son, I know you understand what a gift has been given to you. May you always nurture it, protect it, and help it grow and flourish. And may your love and commitment take you on a long and joyous journey throughout the years to come. Congratulations."

Liz and I raise our glasses to my dad. I watch as Liz mouths to my parents that she loves them. When my dad sat down, her mom starts tapping her glass with a fork, calling attention to herself. She looks to Liz and me with tears shining in her eyes.

"This is hard for me to do," she says quietly. Looking beside her, I see George place his hand against her lower back, and watch her take a breath, his touch giving her strength. "Liz lost her father many years ago, but I know that if he was here, he would have wanted to speak. Liz was always a daddy's girl, and she had him wrapped around her little finger," she laughs. "He used to joke about what life would be like when she started dating, the typical father wanting the perfect man for his little girl." She closed her eyes, and when she opened them again, tears fell. "I truly believe that he sent Trevor to my beautiful baby girl, a man who looks at her like she is the reason he is able to breathe, someone who completes her. I...I'm lucky to call you my son, and thankful that my daughter has a man who I know will always protect and care for her." She raises her glass, and we all follow her lead. "To the bride and groom, my new son and daughter. May you always find a way to overcome challenges together. May you find new ways to fall in love every day all over again. And may your love for each other continue and grow. Cheers." She sits quickly, shoving her face into her napkin, George wrapping his arms around her. I lean over kissing Liz; her lips, nose, and then forehead.

"Can I have the bride and groom make their way to the dance floor for their first dance as husband and wife?" the DJ asks. Adele's Make You Feel My Love starts playing as I take Liz's hand, helping her up, and walking her out to the dance floor.

"I love you, Mrs. Mayson," I whisper into her ear as we sway to the music.

"I love you, Mr. Mayson," she says, looking up at me, her eyes shining brightly with happiness.

"I can't wait to get you out of this dress," I say, running my hands down her sides.

"I think you said that already," she laughs.

"It's all I can think about. It's all I've thought about since you were walking down the aisle to me."

"You look very hot in your tux. I can't believe that you wore one."

"Have you met our mothers, baby?" I ask, looking at her seriously. "If I didn't put the thing on, they would have dressed me themselves."

"You're right; I'm surprised they didn't fuss when I picked my own dress."

"I would have fought them for you." I wrap her closer, one hand on her lower back, the other on the side of her face, holding her close to my body as we continue to sway to the music. When the song ends, my dad takes Liz away from me, while I take Liz's mom's hand for a dance.

"Thank you," she smiles softly, looking up at me.

"For what?"

"Loving my daughter."

"It's easy," I tell her, bending down to kiss her cheek. When the song ends, Liz and I make our way to the table that is holding the cake. Everyone gathers around as we each take a small piece. I feed her the piece I'm holding, making sure that I get it all in her mouth and none on her face. When I bend low for her to give me mine, she touches my nose with it, catching me off guard; my mouth is open, so she shoves the piece in, laughing hysterically then turns to run. But Cash, Asher, and Nico are all blocking her path. Everyone around us starts laughing, and Liz turns back around to face me. I haven't even moved to wipe the icing from my nose.

"Sorry," she laughs. "Um, you have something right here." She points to her nose. I nod in understanding. "Do you want me to get it?" she asks sweetly.

"Come here baby," I say, making sure my voice is the soft but demanding tone that I know drives her crazy.

She shakes her head no.

"Come here." She takes a step towards me, biting her lip. When she gets close enough for me to grab, I lunge, wrapping my arm around her waist. She's bent back over my arm, and I wipe the icing on my nose down her neck, and then proceed to lick it all off her. I listen to her laughing the whole time. "You taste so much better than the cake, baby," I tell her, kissing her lips and hearing everyone applaud.

~~*

"I can't believe this whole place is ours for the next week," Liz says, as we look out over the forest and lake below. After the reception, we got in my truck, and everyone waved glow sticks and threw confetti as we drove away. We had already packed for our week-long honeymoon, our bags in the back of my truck, but we wouldn't need a lot of clothes since I planned on taking advantage of the privacy at our family's Gatlinburg cabin.

"You want to go in the hot tub?"

"Yes, but first I need help getting out of this dress."

"I'm more than happy to help you get out of this dress," I tell her, picking her up and heading inside to the bedroom. Once there, I watch as she pulls a small string that is tied into the waist of her dress, causing the whole bottom half of her dress to drop to the floor at her feet. "Holy shit." I can't take my eyes away. She still has the top of her dress on that looks like a corset. Everything she's wearing is white. In my mind, it contrasts with how unbelievably sexy she looks in her corset, a pair of white silk panties, and white silk stockings with a thick edge of lace that are attached to the garter belt around her hips. A small sliver of skin peaks from in-between her panties and the garter belt, making me salivate.

"Can you untie the back?" She turns around, making me groan. The cheeks of her perfectly round ass are peeking out from the bottom of her silk panties.

"Are you trying to kill me?" I choke out.

"What?" Her head snaps around.

"You seriously have to know how fucking hot you look right now." She gets a crazy little smile on her face before arching her back slightly.

"Can you please untie me?" I step towards her, running my fingers along the edge of her panties on her ass before grabbing one of the ribbons, giving it a gentle tug, and unraveling the bow. When I finally get her completely unlaced, she pulls it around to her front, then places it on the bed, before turning around to face me, her hands holding her breasts. The whole visual is so hot; I actually do know where to start. I pull her forward, my hand wrapping around her hair, bending her head back, giving my mouth access to hers when she gasps. I lick, bite, and suck on her lips, her tongue chasing mine. My mouth travels behind her ear, down her neck to first one breast, pulling her nipple in and sucking hard, then the other, doing the same. Her body arches back. I let go of her hair, drop to my knees, pulling her by the hips so her pussy is right in front of my face, and bite her through her panties, before ripping them to the side and fucking her with my mouth. She grinds down on me, using my head as leverage.

"So fucking wet, baby. You like it when I fuck your pussy with my mouth. You like me eating you." I look up at her, her cheeks flushed, lips pink, and eyes dark and hungry. I grab both her ass cheeks, pulling her tighter against me. "Tell me," I growl.

"Yes, I love it." Fuck, I was going to come in my pants just from watching her get off. I pull her tighter against me, sucking her clit into my mouth. She comes on a scream, and when I know she's back with me, I stand up, kissing her deeply, and start getting undressed with her watching me the whole time. While I pull off my pants, she unclips her garter belt from her stockings and is about to roll them down her thighs, when I stop her.

"Let me do that." I walked over, my fingers traveling up her hips and under the garter belt before pulling her panties down, leaving everything else in place. I help her onto the bed, crawl between her legs, lift one, and then the other, and rest her ankles on my shoulders. I slowly rolled down her stockings, taking my time to kiss every inch of skin I expose along the way. "You're so beautiful." Feeling her wet heat against the head of my cock, I can't help but to slide into her in one long stroke, feeling her wetness surrounding me. Her pussy tightens, her head arches back, baring her neck, and when her eyes come back to mine, I slide out, then back in the same way. Every stroke is slow and precise, making sure to hit that spot that I know will have her screaming when it finally builds up. "You're so tight and wet, baby. I love the way you feel surrounding me." Her arms and legs wrap around me, holding me tightly.

I can feel myself beginning to lose it when I feel her pussy practically begging to convulse around me, each stroke pulling us both closer and closer. "Come with me. Shit, come with me." I put my hand between her legs, pinching her clit and sending her over with me. I rolled over so she was on top of me, both of us breathing deeply. "We just consummated our marriage," I say on a puff of air. She starts laughing, her head coming up.

"We did; now it's official. You're stuck with me, Mr. Mayson."

"Thank fuck." I pull her head back down, kissing the top. "How about the hot tub now?"

"Sure, just let me lay here for a few minutes."

"You can relax in the hot tub." I palm her ass, stand up, and carry her outside to the hot tub. And this is how we spend our honeymoon. Sleeping late, breakfast in bed, lazing around the cabin while reading, watching movies, kayaking on the lake, and nights and days making love.

Chapter 12

"Liz." I can hear my name being called, and I know the voice, but don't know why Kara would be calling my name when I'm on my honeymoon with Trevor.

"Hmm?" I answer from my groggy state.

"Liz." I try to lift my head, but become dizzy from the sharp pain that slices through my head. Then I remember that today is my first day back at work. I was there with Kara when two guys came into the store and forced us at gunpoint out to their van. When I tried to prevent them from taking Kara, something slammed into the back of my head.

"Kara?" I ask, trying to open my eyes; but they seem too heavy, my body to tired. I try to fight against the feeling that is pulling me back under, knowing I need to make sure Kara's okay.

"Liz, you need to wake up." She shakes me and I'm finally able to open my eyes enough to see her standing over me. "Thank God," she says, falling to her knees next to me.

"Are you okay?" I look her over, noticing her clothing intact, and no bruising or scratches are on her.

"Fine...fine." She holds her face in her hands. "After they knocked you out, I didn't try to fight them." She lifts her face, looking at me. "I'm so sorry. They're looking for Tim. I didn't know what to do. I didn't want to, but I told them where he is," she whispers, tears streaming down her cheeks.

"It's okay, calm down." I lift my hand, holding hers. After a few minutes, I'm finally able to sit up. When I look around, I notice that the only light we have is coming from a small battery operated lantern. When I take in our surroundings, I know exactly where we are; well, not exactly, because there are thousands of tornado shelters all over Tennessee, and this one looks like it's been abandoned for a long time. The old cement block walls are disintegrating; the shelves that are supposed to hold supplies are rotten, the smell of mold is so strong that my stomach turns. "How long was I out?"

"I don't know. A while. When they finally stopped, one of the guys took you out of the van, while the other one questioned me about Tim." She starts to cry again, this time, holding her very large stomach.

"Kara, you need to calm down. I know you're upset, but if you go into labor right now, this whole situation is going to go from bad to worse."

"How can I be calm? I just handed over my fiancé to men who want to kill him." She cries harder.

"Kara, I know that you're scared for Tim; but right now, you need to think about you and the baby." I rub her arm, trying to calm her down. "Tim is working with Trevor and his brothers. He is in a better situation than us right now." I remind her of where Tim is at this moment, hoping that it will help to calm her down enough to help me get us out of this hellhole. After a few minutes, her crying stops, and she uncovers her face. "We need to try and get out of here." I tell her, trying to stand. My legs wobble, and I stumble sideways into the wall.

"You're bleeding."

"What?" I ask, leaning against the wall. The back of my head pounds with every beat of my heart. I lift my hand to the back of my head; that's when I feel the large wound and the wetness from my blood against my fingers. When I bring my hand near my face, it's covered with blood. "Shit," I breathe, closing my eyes.

"I'm going to be sick." Kara goes to the corner, throwing up and making my already-queasy stomach lurch. I swallow against the feeling. We both don't need to be sick at the same time; one of us needs to have it together.

"They say head wounds bleed a lot more than any other wound," I say. I'm not sure if I'm saying this for me or for her. She lifts her head, wiping her mouth on the back of her hand, looking at me. "We're going to get out of here, Kara; I promise."

"Okay," she says. I can see how scared she is when she doesn't look at me. Using the wall for balance, I make my way to the set of stairs that lead to the large double doors. Once there, I climb up on my hands and knees to the top, pushing against the doors. They don't budge an inch not that I'm surprised. I scoot down the stairs, sitting at the bottom of the steps, trying to come up with a plan.

"What if we both try?" Kara asks. I lift my head, looking at her standing in front of me; her face is pale, her eyes red from crying.

"We can try." I scoot over, give her room to get up the stairs with me, and once at the top, we both push against the doors, counting and pushing to no avail.

"It's not working," Kara says, making me laugh; the stress of the moment and her words break me down.

"We will get out of here," I say, praying I'm right.

"They took pictures of us."

"What?" I ask, looking over at her.

"When they finally brought me down here," she looks over at me, "they took pictures of us."

"Why?"

"I think they're going to use them to get to Tim."

"We need to find a way out of here," I tell her, and this time my worry seeps into my tone.

"The door won't budge."

"If we can't get out, then we need to find a way to protect ourselves against them when they come back."

"There is nothing in here."

"We can break the old shelves up and use the pieces as a weapon."

"They have guns."

"I know, but either we try to fight, or we wait for them to kill us, or whatever it is they want to do to us." Kara gives me a nod and starts to rub her large belly. "Are you okay?"

"Yes, just some Braxton Hicks. I'll be okay." I watch her closely, praying that my nephew doesn't decide to come into the world right now. "I'm okay; I promise." Kara says, watching me.

"If you start to feel like you're having real contractions, you need to tell me," I tell her, going over to the shelf and using my weight to try and pull it apart. It doesn't budge, so I kick it a few times, but still, nothing. "It's not working," I state the obvious, watching the light flicker and start to dim. "Shit." I run over to the lamp and turn it out, hoping that we will have enough battery when we really need it. "I never even thought about turning the lamp off.

"I never thought of it either."

"You wouldn't happen to have started smoking and have a spare lighter, do you?" I ask Kara, making her laugh.

"No, sorry."

"Figures." We sit there in the dark, my brain running over hundreds of scenarios. I can't believe that yesterday I spent the day driving back home from our honeymoon. After leaving the cabin, we drove to November and Asher's and picked up Lolly; she was so happy to see us and we missed our girl. After we got her, we went home and unpacked, ordered a pizza, and complained about being home and having to go back to the real world. I hated watching Trevor getting ready for work this morning. I wanted so badly to cuddle into him and hide away from the world for a few more days. Now, I wish I would have spent a few more minutes looking at him, kissing him, and telling him how much I love him. When he realizes that Kara and I are missing, he is going to freak the hell out. I'm leaning against the wall when I hear what sounds like a car. I stand when I know it's getting closer.

"Is that a car?" Kara asks, turning on the lamp. I can see the terror in her eyes.

"Kara, I want you to go into the corner, tuck yourself into a ball, and turn off the lamp."

"What are you going to do?"

"I have no idea. Just, please, listen to me. Get in the corner and tuck yourself into a ball." Once I see that she is tucked away and turns off the light, I follow the wall to the opening of the stairs. Listening, I can hear the vehicle stop, then the sound of chain against metal, then the creaking of the door above opening. I see the beam of light from a flashlight shining down the stairs. My heart starts pounding so hard that I hear it in my ears. I hold my breath, waiting for when the person is at the bottom of the stairs, and then I wait patiently for them to notice me. I know it's pointless to try and fight; there are two of them and one of me. They have already proven that they don't mind hitting women. When the light shines around the room, it pauses on Kara for a second, before flying in my direction and shining right in my eyes.

"Liz?" I know that voice. I don't know where from, but I know that voice.

"What do you want?" I ask, shielding my eyes from the bright light.

"I'm here to help."

"Kai?" I ask, realizing who it is. "Do you mind lowering the flashlight?" The light immediately lowers, letting me lower my hands that were shielding my eyes. "What are you doing here? I mean, how did you find us?" I look over my shoulder at Kara, who is now sitting up in the corner.

"Tim helped me out, so I am returning the favor. You're bleeding."

"It has slowed down," I say, touching the back of my head. "How did you find us?"

"Been watching for a while now." He takes a step toward Kara, and I automatically step in front of him.

"I'm just gonna help her off the floor."

"No, I'd rather you not."

"You don't want my help?"

"I never said that. I just need to make sure that you're a good guy."

"Ms. Hayes—"

"Mayson."

"What?"

"Mrs. Mayson...I got married."

"Jesus, you're nuts." He shakes his head, laughing. "As I was saying, Mrs. Mayson, I'm definitely not one of the good guys, but I'm here to help you."

"Why?"

"Your brother gave me what I wanted in exchange for my help."

"Not again."

"No, Mrs. Mayson, you're safe. Now, if you're done, I would like to help Kara off the floor. That can't be good for her or the baby."

"How do you know Kara?"

"I make it my business to know everyone, but in this case, Tim told me. Now, if you would please move." I swallowed; my gut is telling me that he is being honest, but his energy is so scary that I don't know what to do.

"Liz!" Kara cries. I turn around to find her on her hands and knees.

"Oh God, what's wrong?" I run over to her and kneel down.

"I don't think these are Braxton Hicks; I think I'm going into labor." Her breathing is choppy; she cries out again, holding her belly.

"Do you think your water broke?" I ask, rubbing her back.

"I don't think so." I look at Kai, who has knelt down next to us.

"I'm going to pick you up and carry you out of here." Kai gently picks her up, and once we're outside, I take a deep breath, filling my lungs with fresh air. I look around and see a large, black SUV, and a guy who looks like a sumo wrestler standing next to the open driver's side door.

"Any word?" Kai asks the guy, who shakes his head.

"Where is Tim?" I ask, following Kara into the backseat, her face sweaty and pale.

"Don't concern yourself with that right now."

"He will want to be here for Kara." I say softly, watching the sumo guy squash himself behind the wheel.

"We need to get to the hospital."

"I thought you—"

"Remember what I told you, Mrs. Mayson; I'm not a good guy." His voice is so low and gravelly that it sends a chill down my spine.

"Liz," Kara whispers.

"It's okay."

"No, it's not. I think my water just broke."

"Are you sure?"

"That, or I peed on myself."

"Okay." I look around, trying to see how far away we are from the hospital, but there is nothing around, just forest and fields. "Do you know how far from town we are?" I ask anyone who is listening.

"About an hour."

"Oh God," Kara moans, falling across the seat. "I think you should start timing my contractions."

"Why?"

"They're close—too close," she says, breathing deeply.

"What does that mean?"

"IT MEANS I'M HAVING A BABY!" she screams, her face contorting. I wouldn't have been surprised if it did a one-eighty like something from The Exorcist.

"Okay, breathe." I do that crazy breathing thing that I have seen in a few movies. Kara looks ready to kill, but I have no idea how to help her.

"What time is it?" Kara growls. I look at the dash.

"Seven-oh-two," I tell her, grabbing her hand.

"I feel like I need to push."

"Don't push," I say, panicked. Pushing means the baby is coming.

"I have to."

"If you need to push, then you push," Kai says from the front seat. I think it's awfully generous of him, seeing how he's all the way in the front seat, while I'm back here with her. I know that I need to man–up, but I have no idea what to do; and the thought of a baby popping out is making me freak.

"Oh God! Here comes another one!" Kara screams, her head laying against the back door, one foot in the seat, and the other on the floor. "I need to take off my pants."

"What?" I pinch myself to make sure this isn't a very strange bad dream.

"I need to take off my pants. I feel like the baby is coming, so I need to take off my pants," she repeats over and over, every time her voice rises a little bit.

"Okay, I'll help you." I swallow all my personal fears and help her to remove her pants. Kai is in the front seat on the phone. I have no idea who he is talking to, but hopefully it's an ambulance. Mr. Sumo is speeding, but his facial expression hasn't changed since we came out of the tornado shelter.

"Liz, I am really scared."

"Hey, it's going to be okay." I run my hand over her forehead, trying to comfort her.

"It's not going to be ok. I'm going to have a baby in the backseat of a car. I think that might be the definition of not okay."

"Just concentrate on breathing."

"Here comes another one." She shoves her foot into my stomach; my breath leaves me with the pressure. Her other foot is still on the floor. I have the perfect shot of her vag, and I don't want to, but I look down. That's when I see a round something coming out.

"Holy shit," I whisper, looking up at Kara, whose face is bright red. "I can see the head."

"What?" one of the guys from the front seat ask.

"I see the head!" I repeat.

Kara falls back against the door. I rub her knee; the interior lights come on, so I place her pants across her legs so no one else can see what I'm seeing.

"I don't think you have much to go," I say, trying to be encouraging. Kara looks ready to kill me. Her foot goes back in my stomach, this time a little harder than the last, making me grunt in pain. Then she screams so loud that I think my eardrums burst. I look down just in time to see a little face. I look around for something to wrap the baby in. There is nothing, so I rip my shirt off over my head, and hold it out, ready to catch him.

Everything happens so quickly after she pushes that I'm not even sure I remember how the baby got into my arms, just that he is there and crying. Kara is laying back against the door breathing heavily. The cord is still attached, and I know that I need to find a way to tie it off and cut it. That's when I hear the most beautiful sound I have ever heard in my whole life. I look through the windshield and can see the lights of an ambulance racing towards us.

"Thank God," I sigh, as we pull off the road. The ambulance is on the other side. When they open my door and take Kara and my nephew, I feel my first real sense of relief since this day started.

~~*
———

Trevor

"Where the fuck is she?" I put my head between my knees, trying to breathe. Nothing is working. I can't take a full breath. I don't know what I will do if something has happened to her. I look up to see my dad coming down the hall towards me with his phone to his ear. I stand, walking towards him. "Have you heard anything?"

"Liz and Kara are on their way in. An ambulance intercepted a black SUV out on old Spring Place Road. One female gave birth before the ambulance was able to make it to them; the other has suffered a head wound, and is going to need stitches and possibly a transfusion when they arrive." I rub my hands over my face a few times. Knowing that Liz is on her way here gives me a sense of relief; knowing she is hurt has me pacing back and forth in front of the emergency room doors. I need to hold her and see for myself that she is okay. As soon as I see the lights flashing, I run out the doors. The ambulance hasn't even come to a complete stop before I'm pulling the door open. Liz is sitting on the bench; Kara is strapped down in the stretcher, holding a small bundle in her arms. The two EMTs look at me in shock when I climb into the back, pulling Liz into my arms. She is cold and pale, but awake.

"Hi." She starts crying as soon as she speaks. I tuck her face into my neck and hop out of the ambulance.

"Hey, we need—" I turn around, daring him to finish, or to try and take her from me. It will be a long time before I ever let her out of my sight again.

I take a deep breath, the first breath I have taken since I found out that Liz was missing. "I'm just taking her in to the doctor," I tell him, knowing that he's just trying to do his job. As soon as I walk through the emergency room door, the nurse is there, ushering us into a room where she checks Liz over, explaining that her blood pressure is a little low due to blood loss; but everything else looks good. She gives me another blanket for Liz to help warm her up, and says that the doctor shouldn't be too long. I wrap her up and sit in the chair next to the bed. Her hair, chest, and hands are covered in dried blood. I don't know how much of it is hers; I know my dad said that Kara had the baby before the ambulance arrived. "Did they hurt you anywhere else, baby?" I don't want to ask, but I notice that she isn't wearing a shirt. I want to throw up. She shakes her head but doesn't answer. I don't want her to think that I would be upset with her. "You can tell me if they touched you." I lay my forehead against her hand.

"They didn't touch me."

"Where's your shirt?" I whisper, feeling bile crawling up the back of my throat.

"I had to use it to wrap the baby in," she says, running her fingers through my hair. "The only time they touched me was when one of them hit me over the head with his gun because I was trying to make them let Kara go."

"Mr. and Mrs. Mayson?"

"Yes." I stand, wanting to get this over with. I want to take my girl home.

"How's Kara and the baby?" Liz asks.

"They are both doing just fine. After I get you stitched up, you can see them if you want."

"Yes, please."

"Alright. I am going to have you sit on the side of the bed facing your husband." I help her sit on the edge and stand between her legs, my hands under her jaw, and taking comfort in the feel of her skin under my hands and her body close to mine. "I'm going to numb the area. Then I am going to have to shave the area around the wound and clean it up before I start on the stiches." Liz nods, but her eyes fill with tears. I hate seeing her in pain, knowing I can't do anything about it.

"I'm right here." I whisper softly in her ear, rubbing the underside of her jaw. I try to have her focus on me as the doctor turns on a pair of clippers, the sound filling the small room. The nurse comes in, followed by my dad and another officer, who start to ask Liz questions about what happened. The more she talks, the more my blood starts to heat, between what happened with Tim at the job site, and Kara and Liz being kidnapped, I was ready to hurt someone.

"How did Kai know how to find you guys?" Dad asks her.

"He said that he had been watching for a while," Liz answers.

"Did he say why?"

"No." She shakes her head, and I can tell she's lying. "Is my brother okay?"

The other police officer answers, "He's fine. The guys who kidnapped you today went to your brother, showing him a picture of you and Kara. When your brother saw the photo, he attacked one of the guys, overpowering him. The next man pulled a gun and shot your brother at close range in the side. He's awake, and with his wife and son."

"What?" she gasps.

"It's just a flesh wound, Mrs. Mayson." Her body sags in relief when she hears he is all right. "What happened to the guys who took us?"

"Both of them are in custody. Seems they were trying to get your brother to go back with them willingly," Dad says.

"Why?"

"They wanted him to tell the DA that the evidence that your brother had gathered against Max Tavero was all planted."

When the doctor finishes the last of the stitches, I say, "If you don't need anything else, I am going to take her to see her brother, then home." I look at my dad, who nods his head. He hugs Liz, and promises that he and Mom will stop by tomorrow. The nurse comes back in with a top for Liz to wear. I take her into the bathroom and help her get cleaned up. When we make it to Kara's room, Tim is standing outside her door, talking to someone I don't recognize. Liz's hand flexes in mine; her steps falter, putting me on guard.

"That's Kai," Liz whispers.

"Go in the room with Kara and close the door."

"Trevor, he saved us."

"I know, baby, but I'm not going to risk something else happening to you, so do what I say." When we reach the door, I block her as she goes into the room and closes the door behind her. Once I know she is safe, I go in for the kill. I'm not going to have this shit go down again. I shove Kai into the wall, my forearm going into his throat. "What the fuck is going on?" I'm done playing games. I have no idea what he wants from Tim, but I'm going to make it perfectly clear that he is never going to get the information by threatening Liz.

"I'm going to let you get away with touching me this one time because I understand that you're upset about what happened to your wife. But in the future, if you think about touching me, I will end you."

"Do you think I give a fuck? I want to know that I'm not going to have to deal with this shit again."

"I took care of it, Trevor," Tim says, pulling my arm. I step back, shrugging off his touch.

"You took care of it, Tim?" I shove him against the wall. I don't give a fuck that he was shot. "My wife was kidnapped, along with your then-pregnant fiancée, Tim. She delivered your son in the back of an SUV while bleeding from a head wound. You told me that this shit wasn't going to follow you to town. You said that the police were handling everything; so tell me, what the fuck happened?"

"They were going to use Liz and Kara against me. They wanted me to go back with them so that I would agree to talk to the DA. They didn't know that Kai had contacted me already, and informed me of what was going on. He didn't know that the girls were going to be kidnapped, just that they were going to convince me however they had to, to do what they wanted."

"As I was just telling Mr. Hayes, nothing like this will happen again, so he doesn't need to concern himself."

"How do you know that?" All I want to know is that Liz will never have to go through something like she did tonight ever again.

"You never bite the hand that feeds you. Now, I am sure you would like to get back to your families. Tim, thank you again; and congratulations to you and Kara." And with that, he turned and walked off.

"Tim, I need to know that Liz is never going to be in danger again." I run my hands down my face. I had been with Tim at the hospital when I found out that Liz had been taken. I never wanted to feel as helpless as I did in that moment again.

"She won't be." He opened up the door to the room. Kara was sitting up in bed; Liz was in the rocker holding her nephew.

"How's he doing?" Tim asks, walking up to Liz. He runs his hand over her hair, before kissing her forehead.

"He's sleeping," she says, handing him over to Tim, who takes him carefully from her arms. He walks over to the bed where Kara is.

"Let's go home," Liz says softly, grabbing onto my hand.

"Yeah, let's go." I pull her into me, drop her hand, and kiss her. As soon as our tongues touch, I'm lost in the feeling and taste of her. This is what I could never live without; this is what I will always fight for. I pull my mouth from hers, kissing her bottom, then top lip. "Let's go home," I repeat. I kiss her forehead, wrap my hand around hers, and take us home, leaving the day behind us.

Epilogue

One year later.

<u>Liz</u>

"Baby, wake up."

"Trevor, please, I'm trying to sleep. Go away."

"Baby, you need to get up and go to the bathroom."

"I don't need to go to the bathroom!" I cry, shoving my head under the pillow when I feel sleep slipping away from me.

"Baby, I need your first urine."

"What?" I shriek, sitting up and looking at Trevor, who is wearing a white t-shirt, sweats, and a huge smile.

"I need your first urine. Well, that's what this says." He holds a giant piece of paper in front of me, waving it back and forth. I'm following it, trying to see what the hell he is rambling about. "See, it says right here." He points at a small section of writing on the giant piece of paper. "You should use your first morning urine."

"First urine, for what?" I ask confused.

"This!" He holds the pregnancy test in front of my face, making my breath catch.

"Why do you have that?"

"You're late."

"I'm late?" I repeat, not taking my eyes off the test.

"Yeah, we have been having sex practically every day for the last two months. When I first did some research on why you might be late, it said it could be stress, so I wanted to give it some time to see if your period came. It hasn't, so you need to pee on this." He holds the test up again.

"Oh my God," I whisper, feeling a mixture of nerves and excitement. "Baby, you know you're kinda crazy, right? I've never heard of a man keeping track of his wife's period and doing research on it." I smile and stroke my fingers along his strong jaw.

He shrugs. "So?" he says, climbing on top of me, pinning me down to the bed. "You need to get out of bed, wife, and pee on the stick."

"Okay," I smile. His eyes light up as he helps me out of the bed.

"What are you doing?" he asks when I go to shut the door to the bathroom.

"I will be right back."

"I'm going to stay with you." His face is so serious that I start to laugh.

"All I do is pee on it. After that, I will open the door, and you can come in and wait with me while it processes."

"Fine," he grumbles, as I close the door with a giant smile on my face. I didn't even think that we would be doing this so quickly, but with lots of therapy and support from everyone around me, I stopped taking my birth control about three months ago. The day I handed Trevor my pill case was a happy day for both of us. I look down at the test in my hand, and go about taking the test. When I'm finished, I open the door for Trevor, who hasn't moved from right outside it. He comes in, wrapping his arms around my waist. As we wait for the results of whether or not our lives were going to completely change, I hear a ringing and I look at Trevor, who pulls out his phone, turning off the timer. "It said three minutes." He shrugs.

~~*

Trevor

I put my phone back in the pocket of my sweats, and turn Liz around to face me. "No matter what that test says we are in this together," she nods, and I pull her bottom lip out of her teeth. I give her a kiss before grabbing the test off the counter behind her. I hold it between us, and we both look down at the test at the same time. The words PREGNANT is clearly stated through the small window of the test. Her hand goes to her stomach. "We're pregnant," I say, stunned. I mean, I was pretty sure, but you never know. She starts to laugh, making me look up. "What?"

"You said 'we're pregnant'."

"We *are* pregnant," I tell her seriously. "I may not get sick or feel the pain from childbirth, but I will be with you the whole way, taking care of you and making sure that you and our child have everything that you could possibly need." She does a face-plant into my chest, her arms wrapping around my waist. "How are you feeling about this?" I whisper. A few months ago, when she handed me her case of birth control pills, telling me that she was ready for us to start trying to get pregnant, I was worried that she was rushing it because she thought that it was something that I wanted. Later that night, when I was holding her, I expressed my concerns with her. She explained that with counseling and surviving what she and Kara had gone through, she realized how short life really is, and that you can't let your fears rule you. So I got out of bed, tossed the pills in the trash, and went about making love to my wife.

"We're having a baby."

"We are." I kiss her forehead. "I love you, baby.

"I love you most," she whispers, making me smile.

"Let's get you and my kid something to eat. Then we need to call and see about setting up a doctor's appointment."

"Oh, no. Are you going to start freaking out like Asher?"

"If you mean being concerned about you and my child, then yes."

"Please don't buy a baby book."

"I won't."

"Oh, good," she sighs, shaking her head.

"I think I have it memorized from when Asher or Cash had left them hanging around."

She smiles then her smile slips away. "How is Cash going to take this?" she asks, looking at her fingers that are playing with the hem of my shirt.

"He will be happy for us." All my brothers will be.

"I'm happy he's getting a divorce." Liz whispers.

"Me to baby."

"I hate her."

"I know you do. I don't like her much myself, but now that he has custody of Jax things should get better for him."

"I know. Trevor, she was so mean to him. The things she said and did..." She shakes her head, tears start to fill her beautiful eyes.

"Hush, baby. It's okay." I pull her against me again, holding her close. "Let's stop talking about Cash and Jules." I'm fucking happy that Cash finally realized that he couldn't continue to live a lie with Jules. I hate what he went through but I'm glad it's over. The bitch even tried to claim that my nephew wasn't Cash's at one point so Cash had a paternity test done confirming what he already knew. Now they're getting divorced and Cash is getting full custody not that Jules really wanted custody to begin with she just wanted to fuck with Cash. I lead Liz out of the bathroom and into the kitchen. She starts to make coffee. I stand there, trying to figure out how to tell her that she can't drink coffee anymore.

"What do you want for breakfast?" she asks, looking over her shoulder. She looks beautiful in nothing but one of my shirts and a pair of large socks that slouch around her ankles. Her hair is a mess, and the way the sun is shining through the window makes her look like she's glowing; or maybe she is glowing. I can't wait until her waist expands, showing off her pregnancy. I never thought that I could love her any more than I already did. Now, knowing she's carrying my child has elevated every feeling that I have ever had for her.

"Whatever you want, baby," I tell her, when I see her raise her eyebrows.

"How about French toast?"

"That sounds good," I say, watching her fill up the coffee pot with water, worried about what I have to do next.

"Baby, you don't need to make coffee. I'm not going to drink any this morning."

"Its fine," she shrugs. "I'm going to drink it."

"You can't." I cringe, *me*—fucking Trevor Mayson—cringing when giving my slip of a wife the news, afraid of her reaction.

"What do you mean 'I can't'?"

"Well, you're not supposed to drink coffee during a pregnancy."

"You're kidding, right?"

"Nope, you can have decaf though. Just, right now, we don't have any."

"Oh, okay." She turns off the water, going to the fridge, leaving me kind of stunned.

"Are you alright?"

"Fine, just hungry. Can you get my cell phone for me so I can call the doctor and see about setting up an appointment?"

"Absolutely." I smile, thinking that Asher is full of shit. Liz didn't seem to care at all about not having coffee.

~~*

Three months later.

Liz

 "Will you please calm down? You're making me nervous."

"I can't sit down. We're finding out what we're having. What if we're having a girl?"

"Trevor, you know that it's a fifty/fifty chance."

"I know, but I don't know if I could handle having a girl. Look at Asher. He has all girls, and November is pregnant with another one."

"It will be okay."

"I don't feel so well," he grumbles, sitting down next to me. I want to laugh, but I know that he is really afraid about this. I mean, when Asher and November found out that they would be having yet another girl, Asher freaked out. November said that the doctor had to give him something to help calm him.

"Mr. and Mrs. Mayson, if you could come with me," the elderly nurse says, leading us to a room at the end of the hall. "You're going to need to change into this." She hands me a paper robe, and instructs me that once I have it on, I should get up on the bed. Once the door is closed, I start to get undressed. Trevor is frowning the whole time.

"What now?" I ask, exasperated.

"Your doctor is a man."

"Yeah, you know this. You have met him before."

"You never had to get completely naked before."

"He has to check me this time."

"I don't like it."

"I don't like it either, and I'm the one who is going to have someone looking at me down there. So can you please just relax? You're making this harder on me."

"Sorry, baby. I just really don't like people seeing you."

"You do know that when I go into labor, there will be a lot of people in the room."

"Baby," he groans, leaning his head back. "You're not making this any better." I'm laughing when my doctor walks in.

"How are you feeling today, Liz?"

"I'm doing really well." I lean my head to the side, look at Trevor, and smile.

"Good to hear. Today, we're going to be giving you an ultrasound to make sure that everything looks like it should; we can also find out the sex of the baby if you're interested."

"Yes, we would like to know what we're having."

"Good. Well let me just get everything set up, and we will get started." I nod and hold on to Trevor's hand. Once Dr. Spark has everything in order, he has me lay back on the bed, and place my feet in the stirrups. "I need you to relax for me," he says. I do my best and feel a slight pressure down below. Then he stands, putting the samples that he took on the counter, and allows me to lay my legs out straight as he starts spreading a large glob of gel on my small bump. He runs the small device over my stomach, and after a few seconds, the fast swoosh of our baby's heartbeat fills the room.

Trevor holds my hand a little tighter, leaning closer to me so he has a clearer picture of the monitor.

"How does everything look?" Trevor asks, not taking his eyes away from the monitor.

"Well, let me take a few measurements," Dr. Spark says, clicking around on the screen. "From the measurements and the blood that I had taken the other day, everything looks good." He does some more clicking with the mouse and presses around on my belly, before he goes back to looking at the screen. "Alright. Well, let's see if the little guy or girl will cooperate." He keeps running the device all over my belly, then finally he stops. "Well, it seems to me that she is going to be stubborn," he says. It takes me a second to realize what he just said. I look over at Trevor, who is staring at the doctor.

"We're having a girl?"

"You're having a girl," the doctor confirms, smiling.

"Holy shit." Trevor stands, looking closely at the monitor. "You're sure?" he asks the doctor.

"Well, I'm not really supposed to say it, but yes, I'm sure." Dr. Spark laughs, looking between the two of us. "Let me just get you cleaned up. Everything looks great. When you're done getting dressed, just set up your next appointment at the front desk," he says, leaving the room. I sit up, pulling the robe off and tossing it in the garbage. I pick up my sweats off the chair, pulling them on, then sit and start to put on my shoes. That's when I notice that Trevor has been quiet this whole time.

"Are you okay?" I step towards him. When he is able to reach me, he wraps his arms around my waist, kissing my small bump. I run my fingers over his head.

"I thought I would be afraid if he said we were having a girl, but I'm really fucking happy about it."

"I wanted a boy," I tell him.

"You did?"

"I did. I wanted a boy that looked like you."

"You never said anything."

"Well, I knew that I would be happy with whatever we have."

"My daughter is in here." He lifts my tank, his hands spanning my waist.

"She is."

"That's fucking crazy." He smiles up at me, before kissing my belly. "Let's get my girls home."

"Can we stop for ice-cream?"

"Anything you want."

"Anything?"

"Absolutely anything."

~~*

4 months later

Trevor

"Breathe, babe. Breathe." I pull Liz back into me, wrapping myself around her. "You can do this, baby. Just breathe."

"I can't...I can't do this anymore!" she cries. I fucking hate this. We have been here for the last thirty-three hours. She's just now dilated to nine centimeters, and my baby is exhausted. She hasn't really slept since her water broke.

"You can do this."

"I don't think I can." She falls back into me when the contraction passes.

"Alright, hun. I'm gonna check ya and see where you're at so I know if it's time to call the doctor," the older nurse says, lifting the sheet at the end of the bed. After a second, her eyes meet mine, then Liz's. "I do believe it's time."

"Thank you," Liz says, her sweaty face going into my neck. "I'm so tired."

"As soon as this is over, you can sleep. I promise."

"Okay." She says softly. The doctor walks in and sits down at the end of the bed.

"Are you ready for this, Liz?" Dr. Spark asks. I get off the bed from behind her, taking one of her hands. Once everyone is in position, we begin the whole process of pushing. Rita and my mom are on the opposite side of the bed from me. Liz's mom and I each have one of Liz's legs, holding them up to her chest. The doctor is instructing her when to push. Liz bends forward, her face red and sweaty, looking more beautiful than I have ever seen her. I bend forward, whispering encouragements into her ear, and telling her how much I love her. When I hear a very loud cry, and look down and see my daughter, she's covered in blood and slime. Tears come to my eyes, watching her take her first breath. Someone wraps her in a blanket before setting her on Liz's chest.

"You did so amazing, baby." I look down at both my girls...my life.

"She's so tiny, so perfect," Liz whispers, looking at her little fingers. I run my hand along hers, and she latches on to me, her tiny hand gripping my finger firmly.

"I love you, baby girl," I say, leaning in and kissing her blanket covered head, before turning to kiss my wife. "So, are we sticking with Hanna?" I ask, running my finger down her smooth little cheek.

"Yes, I think Hanna fits her perfectly. Don't you?"

"Hanna Star Mayson." I smile, kissing them both again.

"Okay, Mommy and Daddy. We need to take her and get her cleaned up," the nurse says, and I feel torn between staying with Liz, and going with Hanna.

"Can you stay with her?" Liz asks, holding Hanna a little closer against her chest, not wanting to give her up. I'm looking between my two girls when her mom steps forward.

"I'll stay with Liz, honey. You go with your daughter."

"Thanks." I lean in, kissing Liz again, before holding her face in my hands. "Thank you, baby; you did so good." Tears start to slide down her cheeks. Such a drastic contrast from the smile that is lighting up her face.

"We did good," she says, kissing Hanna's head before handing her over to the nurse. I follow Hanna over to the other side of the room, and watch as they unwrap her from the blanket, making her cry immediately. My jaw clenches at the sound, knowing that I have to let them take care of her and there is nothing I can do about her crying until they're done. I look over and see my mom smiling at me; she mouths the words I love you and I close my eyes. I have everything I have ever wanted.

It's been two days since Hanna was born. Two of the most amazing days of my life. Liz is doing great, and regardless of her previous reservations about having a child, she is the most amazing, attentive, and loving mom to our daughter. I look over at Liz, who is asleep. Hanna is laying against my chest, asleep as well. Both of my girls have had a long day, getting released from the hospital, coming home to family wanting to see Hanna and check on Liz, then the blow up between Jules and Cash that had to go down in my living room on the day we got home. It upset not only Liz and Hanna, but Cash and Jules' son Jax, and November and Asher's three girls July, May, and June. I swear my brother is trying to make a full calendar. I have no idea what Cash is going to do, but I know one thing for sure, Jules is a bitch; and if my brother stays with her ass, I'm going to have to limit the time we spend with them.

"You're awake?" Liz asks, leaning up on her elbow.

"Yeah, she just knocked out, so we came to lay down with you. How are you feeling?"

"Sore and a little tired, but good. What time is it?" I turn my head and look at the clock.

"Just after four."

"It's almost time for her to eat again," she says, making me smile. I love watching her feed our daughter.

"Relax, baby. When she wakes up, she can eat. Right now, she's asleep. Didn't the doctor tell you that when she sleeps, so should you?"

"I know. You're right. But I love holding her." She laughs, lying back down. "God, she's going to be as bad as July if we're not careful."

"Baby, I want you to sleep. If she needs you, I will wake you up."

"Fine." She scoots next to me, tucking her face into my side, where I wrap my arm around her, holding her close. "Sleep," I whisper into the top of her head. After a few minutes, her breathing evens out, and I know that she is finally asleep. With both my girls close, I say a small prayer of thanks for all of this.

~~*

One year later

Liz

"Trevor, if you don't stop, you're going to wake Hanna." I bite my lip to keep from crying out.

"No, you're going to wake Hanna." He smirks, his fingers sliding inside me. "Be quiet, baby."

"How can I be quiet when you're doing that?" I breathe, seconds away from coming. "Oh my God! Right there, yesss..." I moan, my head falling back against the mattress. I can feel myself convulse, my orgasm taking over. My back bows, my thighs shake, and my vision goes blurry. When he doesn't let up, I try to scoot up the bed away from his touch.

"Don't run away from me." He pulls me down under him, thrusting into me in one smooth motion.

"God!" I rake my hands down his back, the heels of my feet going to the back of his thighs.

"Da-da... Da-da..." I hear through the baby monitor. I bite my lip, and Trevor's forehead falls against my collarbone. Groaning, he lifts his face. "Da-da..." Hanna sings again, making me laugh and him glare at me.

"What? You bragged for a week about her learning to say da-da before ma–ma," I say, shrugging.

"You think this is funny?" He rolls his hips, making my breath catch.

"No," I say, rocking my hips against his.

"You're gonna get it." He presses me harder into the mattress. "As soon as she's down this afternoon, be ready, baby."

"DA... DA DA DA..." Hanna starts singing, louder this time. Trevor jumps off the bed, his firm ass on full display. He bends, grabs his sweats, and pulls them up, walking into the bathroom. When he comes out, he walks over to the bed, pulling me to the edge. His kiss is so hard that my lips feel bruised when he finally takes his mouth away. I watch as he walks out of the room, the muscles of his back flexing with every step. I fall back against the mattress and listen to him as he talks to Hanna. He is such an amazing father. One-hundred-and-ten percent hands on. There is nothing better than watching him with her, and I'm so happy that I got the help. I needed to give that to him.

"We're ready for breakfast, Mama," Trevor says, standing in the bedroom door. Hanna's sitting on his hip, her hand in her mouth, her head lying against her father's shoulder, watching me.

"Hey, sweet baby." I watch her head come up, and she holds out her arms in my direction for me to take her. I lean forward, grabbing Trevor's shirt from the end of the bed, slipping it on over my head, before swinging my legs over the side, and holding out my arms to take my sweet girl. When I finally have her, she cuddles into me. There is nothing better than moments like this, when she wants to cuddle and be lovey. Now that she has started holding onto things and walking, those times are becoming fewer and fewer, unless she's sleepy or not feeling well.

"Looks like I'm making my girls breakfast this morning." He leans forward, kissing Hanna's and my forehead, before heading out of the room.

"Let's go monitor Daddy. You know what happens when he's left alone in the kitchen making anything besides a protein shake." Hanna laughs, babbling da-da. "You think that's funny?" I lift her, blowing on her soft belly, making her laugh harder as we walk down the hall. Once we reach the kitchen, I see that Trevor has already started making a mess. There's milk, eggs, and a box of pancake mix out on the counter. "Why don't you take her, and I will make breakfast."

"You sure, baby? I don't mind cooking."

"Yeah, she wants you anyways." I hand Hanna over, kissing her all over her face, making her fuss. I love my man, and appreciate when he cooks, but he is seriously messy. It's easier if I cook and clean as I go. I go about making breakfast, while Trevor pulls out Hanna's walker, setting her in it so she can roam around the kitchen and living room. He puts a few Cheerios on her tray; she doesn't eat them, but does feed them to Lolly whenever she is within reaching distance. Every time she gives Lolly a Cheerio, she laughs, pulling her hand back quickly, not sure if she likes the feeling of Lolly's tongue.

"You want some help, baby?" Trevor asks, walking up behind me, his arms wrapping around my waist.

"No thanks. I'm just about done," I say, flipping over the last pancake. His mouth goes to my neck; the scruff from his morning stubble scratches against my skin. "You can't do that right now," I say quietly. His hands flex on my hips, pulling my ass into his hips.

"You smell so good, baby. I just want to eat you." I bite my lip hard, trying not to moan. "As soon as Hanna's down, I'm going to eat you, then fuck your tight, wet pussy until you beg me to stop."

"Trevor..."

"No, you owe me," he growls biting my earlobe, pressing his hips into me, before stepping back and going to Hanna while I finish making breakfast.

"She's down." I jump at the sound of Trevor's voice. I have been trying to catch up on laundry when he walks in.

"Is she okay?"

"Yep, lose the shorts."

"Trevor—"

"I'm not fucking around, baby. Lose the shorts." I can feel myself getting wetter every time he speaks. I shimmy out of my jean shorts, and before they even hit the floor, I'm up on top of the washer. Trevor reaches around me. I hear the washer start, then it is shaking under me. He tears my legs apart, shoving his face between my thighs, attacking me, licking, biting, and sucking. His mouth, and the vibrations from the washer, are bringing me closer and closer to an orgasm. "Ride my tongue, baby. Make yourself come."

"Trevor!" I moan loudly, my pussy convulsing, as billions of colors flash behind my eyelids, my whole body buzzing. He stands and tugs me forward, his mouth meeting mine. I can taste myself on him as he eats my mouth the same way he did my pussy. His fingers sliding inside me brings me closer to another orgasm. I tear my mouth away from his, my head falling back. Then my arms are going up. My shirt is gone, and his mouth is latching onto my breast through my bra, before ripping the cup of my bra down, and picking me up off the washer. He turns me around, my chest going to the cold top of the washer; his thighs spread my legs apart, and he thrusts into me.

"Fuck yes...I have been wanting this all day."

"Harder." My hands go to his ass, pulling him into me.

"You want it hard, baby?" He starts pounding into me so hard that the washer is rocking with the force, and I have to stand on my tiptoes. "I love your pussy; always so tight and warm, baby." His teeth bite into my ear, then my neck. "Touch yourself. I want to feel you come around my dick while I'm fucking your tight little pussy." I whimper. I love his mouth; the things he says are as good as what he does with it. "I feel it. You're gonna come, aren't you?"

"Yesss." I arched my back as he starts pounding even harder. My toes no longer touching the floor. He bites into my neck, pulling out almost all the way, then slamming so hard into me that the washer bangs into the wall, before his strokes slow and he groans into my neck and pulls me slightly away from the washer. We are both covered in sweat and breathing heavily. I lay my forehead against the washer, enjoying the coolness on my overheated skin.

"I needed that," he says against my neck, making me laugh.

"Don't even act like you didn't get some last night."

"That was last night."

"You're crazy," I tell him, looking over my shoulder.

"Love you, baby." My heart melts. I can't believe that my happiness only increases over time. I am truly blessed in the relationship that we have.

"Love you more," I whisper, leaning my head back against him.

"Impossible."

Acknowledgements

First, I want to thank God.

Second, I need to thank my fans. You are all amazing! I couldn't ask for any better; I love you all. Your messages, comments, and love of the Mayson boys has been mind-blowing! Thank you so much.

Next, I need to thank my husband for being my biggest fan and supporter. Your love and encouragement means the world to me, and without you, I would not have followed my heart and started writing.

To my Cookie, thank you for not allowing me to get a fat head. To Sean my brother from another mother thank you for letting me use your apple to write Trevor would not be out without you.

To my mom, you said I had something and to go with it. Love you.

To Mommy and Daddy, thanks for telling me that I can do anything that I put my mind to. I love you both.

I need to give a special thanks to all my family, adoptive and real; your support means so much. I also need to thank Hot Tree Editing. You have been amazing to work with.

A GIANT, over-the-top, crazy-huge Thank You to Kayla Robichaux also known as the amazing Kayla the Bibliophile. You are crazy-awesome, and I am so glad that your side of the brain we share is so smart. I appreciate all your hard work and time that you spent on Until Trevor. Thank you. (And may no one EVER unlock our Snap Chats!)

To each and every blog, reader, and reviewer this wouldn't be anything without you. Thank you for taking a chance on an unknown author. I wish I could name all of you but this would go on forever just know that I love you guys.

To Love Between the Sheets, especially Jennifer, you're awesome! You have no idea how much I have come to count on your advice. Thank you. Last, but not least, to my Beta Readers Jessica, Carrie, Marta, Laura, Jenny, Rochelle and

Midian. I love you ladies. I know I have the best betas in the world. Thank you, girls, for telling me what I need to hear, not what I want to. And thank YOU for loving the men who live in my head as much as I do.

XOXOXOXOXO,

Aurora Rose Reynolds

About the author

Aurora Rose Reynolds is a navy brat whose husband served in the United States Navy. She has lived all over the country but now resides in New York City with her husband and pet fish. She's married to an alpha male that loves her as much as the men in her books love their women. He gives her over the top inspiration every day. In her free time, she reads, writes and enjoys going to the movies with her husband and cookie. She also enjoys taking mini weekend vacations to nowhere, or spends time at home with friends and family. Last but not least, she appreciates every day and admires its beauty.

For more information on books that are in the works or just to say hello, follow me on Facebook

https://www.facebook.com/Aurora-Rose-Reynolds

Goodreads

Goodreadshttp://www.goodreads.com/author/show/7215619.Aurora_Rose_Reynolds?from_search=true

Or Twitter @Auroraroser

Until Lilly

Chapter 1

About four years later.

"Daddy, are we there yet?" Jax moans from the back seat, making me smile. If we're in the car for more than fifteen minutes, he was ready to bust out of his car seat. He has more energy than ten kids combined.

"About fifteen more minutes, dude, then you can go wild." We were on our way to Jumping Bean, a giant warehouse full of trampolines. Hopefully by the time we leave he will be worn out, and I can get some rest. I love my son, but damn if he doesn't wear me out.

"Are you gonna jump wif me?"

"Yeah, dude."

"Yay!" he yells, his little arms shooting straight up in the air. I turn up the volume to the show he's watching hoping that it will keep him occupied until we get to the warehouse. When I found out that Jules was pregnant, I was pissed off at the world. I was in love with Lilly. I hated saying goodbye to her. I knew that in order to have a relationship with my child, to have my child in my life, I had to cut her out and focus on Jules. After a year, I realized that it would never happen. I was killing myself to make someone happy that never would be. Almost three years ago, we divorced and she moved into an apartment in town. My son stays with me unless I am at work. Then my mother, November or Liz has him. His mother sees him if the mood strikes, which is rare and perfectly fine with me, but difficult for him.

"Are we there yet?" I chuckle, shifting lanes as I exit the high way.

"Two minutes."

"This is taking forevvvverrr," he sighs. I look at him through the rearview mirror. His head is resting on his fist, looking completely disgruntled.

"Look." I point out the front window to the building ahead of us.

"We should mobe here." he says.

"Wouldn't you miss grandma?" I pull into the parking lot and find a space to park.

"Well, she could come, too."

"I don't think grandpa would like that, little dude."

"Eberyone could mobe here." I shake my head, getting out of the truck. By the time I have his door open, he unbuckled himself and launched his little body at me.

"You ready to go have some fun?" I hold him upside down, his laughter making me laugh.

"Yes-s-s-s-s." He screeches as I bounce him. I turn him upright, putting his baseball hat on his head like me he always wears one. I grab his hand as we walk into the building. This place is insane! There are kids everywhere, running and screaming, chasing each other when we stop at the front counter to pay. "I wanna go in there, Daddy." I look to see he's pointing at a giant pit full of foam blocks. I am sure it looks like a good time to a kid, but to me as a parent it looks like a petri dish. I am going to have to wash him down with Purell by the time the day is over.

"We will." He nods in agreement. I pull off his hat, and we both take off our shoes before putting them in one of the cubbies that take up a long wall. When his shoes are off, my little dare devil takes a running start, jumping in full speed head first into the pit. I laugh, watching as he tries to right himself.

"Come in, Daddy." He tries to wave, but he looks like a fish out of water flopping all over the place. I step into the pit once I reach him I lift him above my head, and I toss him making him laugh harder. He somehow manages to get his feet under him and wades toward me looking like he is fighting a hard current. "Let's go ober there." He points to a large trampoline that is built into the ground before taking my hand, leading the way out of the pit. I don't know who is going to be more exhausted by the time this day is over. Actually I do, and I know it won't be him. As soon as were out of the pit, he takes off on a run before bouncing onto the trampoline. I stand off to the side, watching him with my arms crossed over my chest. I look to the left when I see a flash of red hair in my peripheral vision. It wouldn't be the first time my mind has played a trick on me making me think I see Lilly when I don't. The woman has fuller hips then Lilly did, her ass is round, making me want to slap it. Shit I need to get laid. The thought leaves just as quickly as it comes. My focus is my son. My bachelor days are a long forgotten memory. Now if I need to get off I use Miss. Right or Miss. Left. I'm just about to look away when the woman turns towards me and I stop breathing. I swear to god time stops. All I can do is stare at her. Her skin is still the color of cream, her red hair is long and hangs over her breasts that seem to be larger than when I last had them in my hands. She looks even more beautiful if that's possible. When her eyes meet mine she blinks then pales, her hand covering her mouth. What the fuck?

"Mommy, Mommy." She looks down, and my stomach drops a little girl with dark hair pulled into two pigtails and skin the same color as her mom's. Lilly gets down to the little girl's level, pulling her close as she whispers something to her. "I don't wanna weabe." She cries, her face turning towards me. For the second time in as many minutes my world comes to a halt. She looks so much like Jax that they could be twins. I look up, my eyes meeting Lilly's again."

"Daddy, come play with me." Jax grabs onto my pant leg. I look down at him, then back at Lilly as tears pool in her eyes. She picks up her daughter, our daughter, and starts to take a step away. Automatically, my hand reaches out to grab onto her elbow. I look down at Jax and give him a smile. "You go play, dude. I will be there in a second."

"Fine." He grumbles before running off again. I look at the little girl in Lilly's arms, her eyes are on me as she leans in to whisper something into her mother's ear. Lilly closes her eyes, hugging her tighter before saying something back to her and setting her on the ground.

"Go play for a minute, love bug." Lilly tells her. The little girl doesn't take her eyes off me. I want to pick her up and hold her so badly that my fist clench fighting it. Lilly kisses her forehead before turning her towards the trampoline. I watch her walk away then start to bounce. It takes a second for my brain to start functioning.

"That's my daughter!" My blood starts to boil. She kept her from me.

"No, that's my daughter." She takes a step to the side away from the other adults around us. I follow, standing at an angle so I can watch my kids.

"I can't believe that you would keep my kid from me." I look her over, the feeling of hate consuming me.

"You're a piece of work you know that? Your words were, get rid of it, that you were getting married and having a baby with someone else."

"What?"

"I read those words over and over a hundred fucking times, so don't tell me that she's yours." She pokes my chest, getting in my space. "She is mine! I suffered from morning sickness alone. I went to my doctor's appointments alone. I was in labor for forty-seven hours alone, and I've raised her alone." She growls the last words. At this time I have no idea what the fuck she is talking about.

"I never told you to get rid of my child, so don't even try that shit with me."

"Oh, yeah? You did buddy. I even printed the text messages you sent me. I kept them as a reminder to myself to never trust a man again."

"I don't know what the fuck you're talking about." I say. I can feel a sinking feeling taking over my body.

"The day I found out I was pregnant; I messaged you telling you that we needed to talk. You said we had nothing to talk about. I said we did, and you said we didn't again. I told you I was having your child, and you told me to get rid of it."

"Oh, fuck!" I rub my face, knowing this is all Jules. She did this, somehow she did this. "It wasn't me." My voice is gruff to my ears. For the first time in years I want to cry like a little bitch. She's watching me closely, her arms wrapped around her waist, her expression changing from anger to confusion and sadness. "What's her name?" I ask, looking at my daughter who is now talking to Jax. He grabs her hands, bouncing with her.

"Ashlyn Alexandra." This is killing me. She gave her a version of my middle name. I swallow the lump that is building in my throat. I look at Lilly.

 "I want it back." I don't even realize that I say the words out loud. Lilly was my one, and I lost it and was going to get it back. I had wanted to search for Lilly a million times. I was so afraid that she wouldn't want me back, accept Jax, or that she had moved on, I talked myself out of it every time. Now I wish I would have looked for her.

"What?" her eyebrows draw together in confusion, the same way they used to when we were together, making her look adorable.

"We are going to have to figure out a way for me to be in her life, and for her to know her brother." I take a step towards Lilly. "Where are you living?"

Her eyes get bigger, and her breathing picks up. Fuck yeah, I still affect her. "Um, we just moved to Springhill because I got a teaching job." She says quietly, while looking at Ashlyn and then back at me.

"Good, you're not far from me." She starts shaking her head. I bring my hand up, cupping her cheek. "We will figure out a time to meet. We have a lot to talk about, but right now let's just have a good time. I don't want the kids to get freaked."

"Ashlyn is already freaked. She knows who you are."

"What?'

"The pictures that we took with my cell phone. She has them, and she knows who you are."

"Jesus." I rub the back of my head. "Where did you say I was?"

"Here."

"Here?"

"Yes, well." She pauses, clearing her throat. "We lived in Alaska near my parents up until a few months ago when I got the teaching job."

"So you told her I lived in Tennessee?" I look over at where Jax and Ashlyn are laughing with their little legs moving rapidly as they bounce in place.

"My dad wanted me to tell her that you were dead, but I couldn't do it." She whispers, and my head swings back in her direction.

"Why didn't you try harder to get a hold of me?" I rip my hand through my hair. This situation is completely fucked up.

"Why the hell would I do that when you told me to have an abortion?"

"That wasn't me," I growl

"It was your phone." She shakes her head. "So you never got married?" She rolls her eyes. "Obviously, you had a son." She points at Jax.

I did not want to answer that question. I knew the minute I told her I had been married that she wouldn't believe that I never told her to have an abortion either. She must have read the look on my face. When she answers, her words are so soft and full of pain that I swear I can feel them cut into my skin.

"I already know that you got married, so even without you answering that question I still know." I see pain flash across her face. "I didn't want to believe that what we had could be so easily replaced. I thought that I had done something wrong, and you were upset. I thought you loved me. I was depressed and lonely, so I did a search of your name online planning to come find you, and came across your wedding announcement."

"What the fuck?"

"Yeah, that is kinda how I felt." She gives a slight laugh, the kind that isn't of humor.

'I am so sorry, you will never be on your own again." I tell her, taking a step towards her because I want to hold her. She takes a step back, shaking her head.

"We can figure out a way for you to be in Ashlyn's life, but only if you plan on sticking around. I won't let her become attached to you and only to have you walk away without an explanation."

"I would never do that." I narrow my eyes and she raises her eyebrows crossing her arms over her chest.

"You are the one who taught me the meaning of never say never?" She reminds me. I told her never say never when we first got together. She told me she wouldn't sleep with me ever, and I told her never say never. We only slept together one time. But that one time had made me fall more in love with her than I already was. The day after, I had to come back home and go back to work.

I never knew that would be the last time I would see Lilly. I knew then that she was the one for me, even as young as I was. I knew, and in the end I tossed her away thinking that I was doing the right thing, but not knowing how sharp the double edged sword was that I had in my hand. We both stand there staring at each other. I don't know what she's thinking, but I'm thinking that I want to kiss the fuck out of her, hold her, love her, and remind her of how good we were together. She looks away, then waves for Ashlyn to come to her. I watch my daughter bounce all the way over to where we're standing. She is so beautiful that my chest hurts looking at her. I have loved every second of raising my son, and I hate that I have missed so much time with her. Jax comes along with Ashlyn. When she reaches where we're standing, her head goes way back with her cute little face scrunching up.

"Are you my daddy?"

"No, he's my daddy." Jax launches himself at me. Ashlyn looks at Jax and then me. I drop to my knees in front of her, putting my arm around Jax's waist. I have no idea how to handle this right now, and my stomach starts to turn as my palms begin to sweat.

"Come here, love bug." Lilly pulls Ashlyn into her arms.

"Daddy." Jax puts his palm on my cheek, forcing my head to turn. "Why did that girl ask if you're her daddy?" Leave it to a kid to get right to the point.

"Well... Um." Fuck, why couldn't I think of what to say?

"What's your name, honey?" Lilly asks. I look up to see Ashlyn in her arms looking down at us.

"Jax." Lilly smiles so bright her whole face lights up. I forgot that smile. How the fuck did I forget that smile?

"Very cool name." Jax chest puffs out under her praise.

"I'm going to be big like my daddy." He informs her randomly.

"I'm sure you are, honey." Lilly smiles again. "How would you feel about having a play date with Ashlyn sometime?" Jax shrugs. I look at Ashlyn who smiles. "Sure, she could come to my house I have a ferret and a tree house."

"I'm sure she would like that, though I'm not sure what a ferret is." Jax laughs and so does Ashlyn. I can't believe how much they look alike. "I'm going to get your dad's number, and we can set up a time."

"Yay!" Jax yells jumping up and down.

"Will you do me a favor, Jax?" He nods. "Take Ashlyn over to get her shoes while I get your dad's number?"

"Okay." He agrees right away. Lilly sets Ashlyn down. She hasn't taken her eyes off me. Jax takes her hand, pulling her along. I watch as she shows him where her shoes are. They are too high for her to reach, so he gets them for her then runs and grabs his before sitting next to her on the ground.

"I think it's best if we talk to them separately about what's going on. Jax is going to be very confused about this, and Ashlyn isn't going to be much better off. She knows of you but doesn't know you. I think we should set up a time for you to come alone and spend some time with her, then bring Jax along later so they can get to know each other."

"Why are you acting so cool about all of this?"

"I don't know. I guess I will save my break down for tonight when Ashlyn is in bed, and I can have a glass of wine." She pulls out her cell phone from her back pocket, sliding a finger across the screen. "So what's your number?" I rattle it off, watching as she types in the numbers. My phone starts ringing from my pocket. I pull it out and save her number quickly. She turns her back on me, walking to where the kids are sitting.

She runs her hands over Jax's hair before grabbing her shoes. She bends over, putting them on with her round ass in the air. I look around when I feel a sting against my skin, my eyes landing on a guy who is looking right at her ass with his wife or girlfriend standing right next to him. I walk up to where Lilly is bent over, not taking my eyes off the guy who is watching her. When I get there, the guy's eyes come to me, and I give him a chin lift. He looks away quickly, making me feel somewhat better. I still have the urge to shove a foam block down his throat.

When Lilly finally stands, I grab my shoes and hat after pulling on my sneakers. I put my hat on, shoving my hand in my pocket so I can grab my keys. I turn around to see Lilly looking at me funny, Jax holding one hand and Ashlyn holding the other. My heart squeezes at the sight of them together. She blinks, shaking her head. "You ready?" I ask, "Yeah." Lilly nods. Jax lets go of her hand and runs to me, grabbing mine. We wait and hold the door open for them.

"Your hair is really red." Jax say looking at Lilly. She laughs shaking her head. The sun is out shinning down on her, making her red hair shine more brightly, giving her a glow.

"She just colored it. It was brown before." Ashlyn informs us, making me laugh as I'm thinking that the last time I saw her, her hair was the same color it is now only a lot shorter. We walk out to the parking lot, and Lilly stops at a small piece of shit car. The once silver is grey and dull with rust stops and dents. She opens the back door, and Ashlyn crawls inside. I don't like this. My body is fighting itself not wanting them out of my sight.

"So I will call and set up a time with you."

"Call me when you get home." I tell her, my voice rough with anger, not at her but myself. She shakes her head.

"No. I'll call you in a couple days after you have had some time to think about this." I take a step towards her, getting in her space.

"I am not going to change my mind." I growl the words, making her eyes widen slightly. Then she takes a breath.

"Well then call when you're ready." She says quietly before squatting down to Jax's level.

"It was very nice to meet you, Jax." She holds out her hand for a shake.

"You're pretty like my mom." Jax was wrong. Jules is pretty, but so rotten on the inside that it has started seeping out making a once pretty girl ugly. Now Lilly, Lilly is more than beautiful and if the situation between us hadn't made her bitter, then nothing ever would. And I could see her light shine through every time she looked at our daughter.

"Well thank you honey." She gave a small smile before standing back up and opening her door. I leaned in the back door so that I could talk to Ashlyn.

"I will see you soon, okay?" She nods. Her eyes are big and the same color as mine.

"So are you my daddy?" She ask more quietly this time.

"Yes." I whisper running my hand over her hair.

"Why didn't you come see me?" Oh god this was killing me. I had no idea how to explain this to her. I didn't even know how to explain this to myself.

"I am so sorry baby." The words choke out. "I promise you that I will come see you now every chance I get."

"Grandpa says that you habe to keep your promises."

"He is right." I smile at the way she pronounces her v's the same way as Jax. "You do have to keep your promises." She nods in agreement. "I'll call your mommy later and say goodnight to you."

"Okay." She reaches over, grabbing a small doll and holding it in her lap. I lean in a little, kissing the top of her

430

head. I get out of the car and see that Lilly and Jax are talking.

"You ready, little dude?" I look down at Jax who is watching Ashlyn curiously.

"I'm hungry."

"You're always hungry." I laugh, watching Lilly get in the car. She shuts the door turning her car on before rolling down the window.

"Grandma says I'm growing."

"You are. Soon you're going to be taller than me."

"Wow." His face lights up.

"But you have to eat your vegetables."

"I don't want to be as tall as you." He grumbles, and I pick him up tossing him over my shoulder chuckling.

"Sure you do." I look at Lilly who is watching me with a small smile. We'll talk soon." She nods. "Call me when you get home." I tell her

"Cash."

"Lilly, call me when you get home." I say it a little slower so she knows I am not fucking around. She shakes her head.

"I will message you," she sighs.

"No, no more messages. Call me." Her eyes flash like they used to when we were a couple and her temper would flare. I used to love when it happened. I would kiss her until she melted into me and couldn't remember why she was mad.

"Fine, I will call you." She rolls her eyes, making me want to fist her hair and put my mouth on hers.

"Say bye, love bug." Ashlyn waves from the back seat and Lilly from the front as I set Jax down next to me. We watch Lilly and Ashlyn pull out of the parking lot. I don't like the feeling coursing through me. I don't like them driving away, and I don't like the amount of hate that I am feeling towards Jules. I didn't think I could hate her more than I did, but she proved me wrong. I needed to call my brothers. I needed to talk to them and have a beer.

"How about we stop at grandmas?"

"Okay." Jax shrugs. I can tell he's getting tired and will most likely be asleep by the time we hit the highway. After I get Jax in the car and buckled in, I hop behind the wheel and I send a text to each of my brothers telling them to meet me at the barn in an hour. I can't believe that Jules told Lilly to get an abortion.

The whole time she was pregnant she threatened to have one if I didn't do exactly what she wanted. I shake my head and put my truck in reverse. Stare at myself in the mirror and notice my hat, it's the same hat that Lilly gave me when we were dating. Yeah, I haven't stopped wearing it since then. I head out of the parking lot wondering if this is my time, wondering if I was finally going to have a chance to be happy again.

Printed in Great Britain
by Amazon.co.uk, Ltd.,
Marston Gate.